NEGOTIATING
TACTICS

Wyvern Crest
Publications

Published by

Wyvern Crest Publications
A Division of
Wyvern Crest Limited
Wyvern House
6 The Business Park
Ely
Cambs
CB7 4JW
01353 665522

First published in 1997

© Wyvern Crest Limited 1997

British Library Cataloguing in Publication Data
A catalogue record for this book is available from the British Library

ISBN 1 899206 11 6

Text design by Lisa Alderson
Typeset by Pantek Arts, Maidstone, Kent.
Printed by Bell and Bain Limited, Glasgow.

NEGOTIATING TACTICS

A portfolio of winning tactics

Negotiations are one of the trickiest situations that managers have to face. Professional negotiators possess a portfolio of dynamic tactics and techniques, and can virtually guarantee that they will always win. But when it comes to it, how sure are you about winning your next negotiation? Do you know how to handle the unscrupulous person who tries to pull a fast one over you? Let's face it, there are occasions when we could all do with having just a few more tactics up our sleeve.

Negotiating Tactics, which pools together the expertise of 12 experienced negotiators (including one who has experienced kidnap and siege situations), is designed to give you those key tactics that make all the difference. It focuses on what you can do to influence each negotiation and is packed with practical ploys for handling almost any situation. Divided into ten chapters, it takes you through over 70 different negotiating tactics.

Bluffs, red herrings and lies

If it's bluffs, red herrings and lies that you want to know about, chapter two has the answers: including questions that can expose an opponent; loaded questions and ways of flushing out the lies.

Smokescreens and tricky trades are common ploys of the professional negotiator. Do you know how to 'split the difference' successfully? What should you look for in the trade-off game? How can you inflate your influence, even when you think you are the underdog? All these tactics, and more, are explained.

The negotiator's secret weapon

Body language is the secret weapon in the professional negotiator's armoury. Most of us tend to overlook it, but it is undoubtedly a highly effective tool. When it comes to spotting signals and reading your opponent without a word passing between you, body language says it all.

Next to the subtle tactics are those that surprise. No one likes to be caught in an ambush but, as every military tactician will tell you, a surprise attack is often what makes the difference between success and failure. Whether you want to use it on someone or learn how to handle a surprise when it's used on you, the tactics here give you all that you need.

Dirty and devious tactics

It would be nice to think that everyone in business is straightforward and decent. And while the vast majority of people are, just occasionally you will meet someone who is downright devious and dirty. If you find yourself up against one of these characters, here's how to foil them.

When it's not a dirty or devious trick that's being played, then someone's bound to try using an ultimatum that's designed to make you sweat. It may be that you encounter an arrogant know-it-all or someone who is making veiled threats. With the solutions in chapter nine, though, it'll seem like water off a duck's back.

So, whether your deal is worth £200 or £2 million, *Negotiating Tactics* gives you the edge when closing deals and influencing others. It's an outstanding short-cut to handling any negotiation. And, since we are negotiating almost every day of our lives, it's an investment that will repay itself time and again.

Packed with examples

Each tactic is explained thoroughly: what you have to do to make it work and the kind of traps that you need to avoid when using it. Copious examples, many from real-life situations, show you how the tactics work in practice.

Time-saving checklists for getting it right

If you're pushed for time you may not be able to scan every word of every tactic, which is why each one contains a quick-reference checklist, summarising the key points.

In a competitive world, in which you need to be alert to every trick that people might pull on you, *Negotiating Tactics* gives you *the* resource to get what you want, when you want it.

iv

CONTENTS

3	SUBTLE SMOKESCREENS AND TRICKY TRADES

4	BOTTLENECKS AND BODY LANGUAGE

5	**NICE SURPRISES**

6	**DEVIOUS AND DIRTY TACTICS**

7 | SNARES AND AMBUSHES

8   GAINING THE EDGE

9   SWEAT TACTICS AND ULTIMATUMS

10 | WHEN YOUR BACK IS TO THE WALL

CONTRIBUTORS

Mike Brookes
BA MBA
MIPD MIMgt

After completing a BA honours degree at Liverpool University in English and History, Mike joined the Royal Air Force in 1959. Before attending Staff College at Bracknell, he worked in training and personnel at home and overseas. Subsequently, he moved into line management and staffwork.

Mike is now employed as the Deputy Director of the Eastern, Essex and Hertfordshire Regional Employers' Organisation, charged with providing services to 54 local government authorities. These services embrace industrial relations, employment law, training and management development. Married and living in Norfolk, Mike spends a good proportion of his spare time in France.

David Crosby BA

David has spent the last ten years in business publishing, working on many successful publications, including the influential *Financial Times* and *Institute of Management* series. In that time, he has edited, crafted and contributed to several hundred leading business and management titles. He is currently Publisher at Wyvern Crest Publications and a regular contributor to the fortnightly newsletter, *Business Now*. He has successfully concluded hundreds of tricky contractual negotiations, many of them pitched against some of the best legal minds.

Anne
Fanning BA

Anne Fanning has been negotiating commercially for over twenty years. In that time, she has met and dealt with almost every dirty negotiating trick in the book. Her stint with a Regional Health Authority during one of the NHS restructurings was particularly instructive. She regularly gives training presentations in the field of direct and database marketing and these always contain advice on negotiating.

She is currently Marketing Director at Wyvern Crest Ltd, with particular responsibilities for the sale of rights. This is rapidly expanding her understanding of negotiating with other cultures – an experience she meets with a certain relish. "Negotiating can be hard work if you don't enjoy it and you can't always deal with people who make it pleasant. But if you look, you can usually find fun in most negotiations, and that is when you will be most successful."

Patrick Forsyth

Patrick Forsyth runs Touchstone Training & Consultancy, based in London. A consultant with some twenty years' experience, he specialises in the marketing, sales and communications area. His training work involves public seminars for such organisations as management institutes, tailored in-company courses and work on training materials in workbook, video and audio form. He works across a variety of industries and regularly works internationally. He is the author of a number of successful business books including: *Making Successful Presentations* (Sheldon), *101 Ways to Increase Sales* (Kogan Page), and *First Things First* – on time-management –

(Pitman). He has also written, on this subject: *Conducting Effective Negotiations* and *The Negotiator's Pocketbook*. He can be contacted at Touchstone Training and Consultancy, 17 Clocktower Mews, London, N1 7BB. Tel. +44 [0]171 226 5949.

David Hentsell

With a background in sales and marketing, working for a number of blue-chip corporations, David Hentsell has a dynamic and varied international career. At one stage, he was responsible for the successful running of no less that 14 five-star hotels in the Middle East. Invited to join a European management consultancy, David progressed rapidly to Regional Director.

David is now a Director of Results International plc. Results International plc is a collaboration between Peter Thomson, the UK's leading personal and corporate-development strategist, and Nightingale Conant, the world's leading publisher of audio-learning programmes.

Results International plc, P.O. Box 666 Leamington Spa, Warwickshire, United Kingdom, CV32 6YP. Tel: +44 [0]1926 339901 Fax: +44 [0]1926 339139. David's direct line: +44[0]1420 472522.

Matthew Hunter

Matthew Hunter studied at the School of Oriental and African Studies and has spent the past 20 years working in project- and export-management. He has worked in the Middle East and has travelled extensively throughout Japan, Korea, south-east Asia and the United States. In 1986 he started his own consultancy company and now helps several major UK companies develop their management and shop-floor teams. He runs negotiation workshops all over the UK and is currently involved in working with management and trade union councils. He is on the Institute of Export specialists register and is a member of the Institute of Personnel and Development. Matthew lives in Banbury with his wife and two children. He can be contacted on +44 [0]1295 252765.

Pat Kilbey

Business writer and journalist Pat Kilbey says she learned the art of negotiation the hard way – through practice. Qualifying as a journalist in the 1970s, she moved on to head her own successful business for 12 years, before deciding to go back to writing full time. Currently, Pat is editor of the subscription newsletter, *Business Now*, which offers a wealth of down-to-earth, practical advice to company directors and managers. She also produces and edits *Book-Talk*, a business-book review service on cassette.

Dr John Potter

Dr John Potter is an international management consultant, advising a range of blue-chip clients on leadership, negotiation and managing pressure in the work place. For some years, he has been involved in training negotiators in both commercial and hostage-negotiation situations and has been operationally involved in a number of kidnap and siege situations.

John is now a director of Results International plc. Results International plc is a collaboration between Peter Thomson, the UK's leading personal and corporate development strategist, and Nightingale Conant, the world's leading publisher of audio learning programmes.

Results International plc, P.O. Box 666, Leamington Spa, Warwickshire, United Kingdom, CV32 6YP. Tel: +44 [0]1926 339901 Fax: +44 [0]1926 339139.

Brian Robinson   At first sight he seems multi-faceted: personal coach and trouble-shooter in public speaking and communication skills, to the directors of some of Britain's best-known companies; holder of seminars in team-building, media studies, etc.; broadcaster; writer, BBC Radio Arts Producer; Theatre Director, etc. – the list seems so disparate. But it is all communication. Brian is obsessed by the magic that makes communication succeed. Whether working through his training/production company, *Auracle*, spending his Saturday mornings directing school children in a play, or transmitting his Sunday BBC Radio Suffolk Arts programme, *Preview*, Brian is working with communication all the time. He can be contacted on +44[0]1638 780668.

Barry Sadler   Barry Sadler started his career with a leasing brokerage. After spending three years as a salesman he took the position of sales manager, leading a 35-strong team to become the largest leasing brokerage in Europe. That company went on to write its own lease book and Barry was instrumental in the setting up and operation of funding lines totalling millions of pounds.

Barry then left that company and opened his own private leasing company and also started a training and consultancy business with a partner. That company has been responsible for training hundreds of sales people throughout the country, using its open courses and audio tapes programme.

Peter Thomson   With more than twenty years' experience in building and selling a variety of businesses, his last for £4.2 million to a major plc, Peter Thomson is now regarded as the UK's leading personal and corporate development strategist. His highly interactive in-house and public seminars are illuminated by the wit and wisdom that only comes from wide business experience.

Peter has collaborated with Nightingale Conant to form a new company, Results International plc, of which he is chairman. Results International plc is an unprecedented meeting of minds in the field of business growth and personal development. The company brings together a range of people successful in a multitude of disciplines, with diverse experiences and international reputations.

Results International plc, P.O. Box 666, Leamington Spa, Warwickshire, United Kingdom, CV32 6YP. Tel: +44 [0]1926 339901 Fax: +44 [0]1926 339139.

Matthew Wright After graduating from Leeds University with a Masters in International Communications, Matthew went on to join a major international information technology company. With his deep understanding of the processes behind effective communications, Matthew quickly established himself as a communications consultant within the business, advising on policy and strategy at a European level.

Matthew is now a Director of Results International plc. Results International plc is a collaboration between Peter Thomson, the UK's leading personal and corporate development strategist, and Nightingale Conant, the world's leading publisher of audio learning programmes.

Results International plc, P.O. Box 666, Leamington Spa, Warwickshire, United Kingdom, CV32 6YP. Tel: +44 [0]1926 339901 Fax: +44 [0]1926 339139.

1 | STRONG STARTS AND TOUGH TESTS

1 | HOW TO FIRE THE OPENING SHOTS

'...there is no 'right' way to begin...'

Many people are unsure about how or where to begin a negotiation. Some people imagine there is a 'right' way to go about it, which will encourage their opponent to respond with a magic 'yes' so that, having agreed, everyone can get up from the table and leave. If only life were that simple! In reality, there is no 'right' way to begin but there are several options to choose from.

The two main openings that you will want to consider are:

- tackling the big issue first;
- the 'softly, softly' approach, to build mutual trust and co-operation.

What may happen if you go in with your guns blazing

The first strategy here is a fairly high-risk one. If you go in with big demands on the most contentious issue first, you may provoke the opposition, with the result that the negotiations fall at the first hurdle. You may also cause your opponent to think "if it's this difficult at the start, *what* is it going to be like later on?" They may not appreciate that this issue will necessarily be the most difficult one. On the other hand, if the issue is contentious, it is by no means certain that a different outcome would be arrived at by leaving it until later on. Dealing with it first may save wasted time in the long run.

Look for the points that bring you closer together

If there are difficult issues to be handled in a negotiation, a safer strategy is to look for points at the outset that bring you closer to your opposite number. This helps to foster an atmosphere of trust and co-operation. It's a bit like meeting someone at a party – you go through the 'getting to know you' stage, find out what their likes and dislikes are and whether your personalities mix together. It's also a very useful information-gathering stage: you can use it to find out the motivations of the other side, which can help you to choose how to handle issues that are raised subsequently. For example, if they agree with a certain principle, you may be able to bring that principle into play later on. It may seem like small-talk, but it can be valuable and, at the same time, generate goodwill. Watch out, though, that the tactic is not being used against you. Are they just trying to soften *you* up, before they become much more aggressive later on? Make sure that with the friendly tone of the proceedings, you are not encouraged to give away key information while they just give away points of no consequence.

Whichever approach you adopt, you will give yourself an advantage if you are the one to kick off the negotiations – it gives you the chance to control the proceedings and sum up points in a light that is favourable to you. Be careful not to disclose your true position when opening a negotiation. Instead, use the opportunity to 'fly a kite' on an issue that is not important. Watch how your opponent reacts. Do they take a hard or soft stance on the issue? Are they being friendly or cold? It may help you decide how to handle the issues of substance.

The way it works   Bill Taylor is the account manager of TDC, a busy print firm in Nottingham. He has been invited by John Thetford, the Director of Anderson's Limited, a company that sells a range of giftware by mail-order, to discuss printing their catalogue, which is produced three times a year. After the initial pleasantries, Bill Taylor leads off by asking John how it was they came to approach TDC. This innocent question opens up a tirade of pent-up complaint about Andersons' previous printers and how these printers let Anderson's down badly, by delivering the order a week later than had been agreed. When the catalogue did finally arrive, the quality was very poor and several pages appeared upside-down. He also divulges that TDC have been recommended to Anderson's by a trusted client.

The opening has given Bill Taylor two pieces of ammunition: firstly, that Anderson's are concerned about quality and service and they may be prepared to pay a premium price for a premium service (he shouldn't have to put in a really low bid to obtain the business). Secondly, because TDC were recommended to Anderson's, there is a good chance that Anderson's will want to try TDC out, rather then choose another printer 'cold'. Bill Taylor can now use this information to sell the quality service that TDC have become known for, with the built-in guarantees of delivering on time and the added security of knowing that TDC have provided a good service for someone else whose opinions are respected.

 ## CHECKLIST FOR GETTING IT RIGHT

✓ Look out for what motivates the other party.
✓ What sort of experiences have they had in the past?
✓ What are their real needs, rather than their desires? Quality or price?
✓ Try and leave controversial issues until later – build rapport first.

'Negotiating strength belongs to the side that is **least anxious** *for the deal to go through.'*

In theory, most negotiations should be evenly balanced: each side wants something and each side has to give something. In practice, this equality is rarely there; one side is always in a stronger position. But which side is stronger has less to do with the facts of the situation and more to do with what each side believes. Negotiating strength belongs to the side that is *least anxious* for the deal to go through. No matter how desperate you are to do the deal, you must create an impression that conceals your desperation and encourages the other side to become more eager to reach an agreement.

For example, a shop may need 200 more mugs to give away as incentives. They have advertised the incentive and have a legal obligation to give the mugs to customers who ask. The factory has thousands of mugs and plenty of people who want to buy them. On this basis, the factory would appear to be in the stronger position. We would expect the shop to be more anxious for the deal to be done than the factory. So the shop's negotiator can and should take steps to make the factory feel more anxious to sell the mugs than the shop is to buy them.

Change the balance of power in your own mind first

Before you do anything else you must work out your BATNA (Best Alternative To a Negotiated Agreement). You must know what you will do if agreement is not reached. Then you must list all the essentials you want (quantity, delivery date, maximum price, colour, etc.). Put these in order of priority, so you are clear in your own mind what trade-offs you can accept: "Yes, we'll accept Royal Blue if you will bring the price down by 3p per unit". Working through your BATNA and your priorities invariably shows you that things are not as desperate as they originally seemed. This helps you present a more relaxed face at the negotiations.

Control the venue and control their assumptions

If the negotiation is to be face to face, try to have it at your office and at your choice of time. Try to avoid lunchtimes, when you would be obliged to become a host: this would reverse the power relationship you established by making them come to see you. Think up ways to imply that their products are less desirable, essential or viable than they think, but that you would still like to buy because they are nice people to do business with. During the negotiations, smile a lot, use relaxed body language, be brisk and businesslike and don't reveal how much you need their products. Behave as though you are confident that they will meet your requirements.

Keep undermining their belief in their position of strength

Don't worry if you are challenged directly on this. Use your BATNA to show that you don't have a problem. For example: Factory: "We know you are out of stock and losing customers: my daughter tried to get her free mug from your Dagenham shop yesterday". Shop: "Yes but it's OK. We are offering people an alternative, which is much more attractive, and most people are

4

leaving with a big smile on their faces! Actually, it's a pity you don't do the Royale design – there is obviously a much greater customer demand for it than yours". In this reply, the shop causes the factory to worry that demand for their product may dry up soon, because a superior product is on the market. The shop is making the factory more anxious to sell.

CHECKLIST FOR GETTING IT RIGHT

✓ Prepare your BATNA and your priorities, before you start the negotiation.
✓ Bring your opponent to your office for the negotiation.
✓ Don't buy them lunch.
✓ Smile a lot and consciously relax.
✓ Be brisk and businesslike.
✓ Early on, introduce the idea that you could get what you want elsewhere, because their product isn't wholly satisfactory, but you prefer to do business with them.

3 | FLOATING AN IDEA, TO EXPLORE THE NEXT STEP

'... that's best for me, whereas ...'

The shortest distance between two points is a straight line. But, in negotiating, the most direct route may not always be the best. How matters are introduced and the way they are described may have a very direct bearing on how they are received. Consider the situation where there are a number of possible options. One must be agreed, and you favour a particular one. How do you make it more likely that your chosen option will be agreed?

People like to win. They measure their negotiating success not only in terms of how the deal stacks up for them at the end of the day, but in terms of how many concessions they have obtained along the way. So, a useful technique is to use one of two or more options as a 'stalking horse'. You make an initial suggestion, with every intention of allowing yourself to be deflected from it. In so doing, you aim to make your preferred option the replacement choice.

Creating a concession

Such a tactic is especially useful when you need to find more points on which you can be seen to concede. By seeming keen on one option and reluctant about another - "... that's best for me, whereas ...." you position what seems to be your preference as something you then abandon, reluctantly. Clearly, depending on circumstances, you can phrase this so that it becomes a minor, or even a major, concession. Thus, this is a technique that can both secure a point you want in your favour and be seen to assist in balancing the overall deal. This assists the overall objective of any negotiation, which is the 'win-win' situation, in which both parties feel they have struck a useful and acceptable bargain.

Avoid overstatement

Like many negotiating techniques, this needs to be used carefully. It is possible to be hoist with your own petard and find that a bogus choice becomes something you are stuck with. However, preparation is again important here, as is experience; this is the kind of ploy with which it is useful to experiment. For example, how you can use it depends, in part, on the range of available options. If there is apparently little to choose between two, say, then greater care needs to be taken to focus ultimate attention on your choice.

The way it works

Mary Stephens works as an account executive in public relations. Like any consultant – anyone selling expertise on a fee basis – she is concerned with productivity as a route to profitability. Time, a finite resource, must be used effectively, if she is to maximise the financial return she brings to the firm for which she works.

She is negotiating the relationship with a new client, a manufacturer whose headquarters are some distance away from her London office. Part of the working arrangement necessitates regular meetings with key staff in the client organisation; these could be at the office of either party.

Mary is conscious that the location of the client reduces productivity (even if travel expenses are paid, and some of the time covered, she has other things to do). But she also knows that the relationship is in the nature of an experiment for the client; they want it to work but are concerned about a new area of, seemingly rather open-ended, cost.

Use a 'stalking horse' Having got agreement to the need for the meetings involved, Mary therefore starts by apparently rejecting the thought of London meetings: "You won't want to come all the way to town, so ..." and suggests that the natural place for such meetings is at the client's office: "... this would certainly be most convenient for you, and the costs involved are allowed in our proposals". With subtle phrasing and prompting such as this she can ensure the point about costs is picked up: "Hang on, just how much are we talking about in terms of cost?". Then it is an easy matter to switch the emphasis, maybe seemingly reluctantly, to the even greater advantage of having meetings in London "Well, I suppose that might work ... we can set dates to tie in with other business to save you an extra journey", and obtain agreement to exactly what she wants. Thus she can service the account efficiently and still have time enough for her other priorities; a solution with which both parties feel happy.

CHECKLIST FOR GETTING IT RIGHT

✓ Make sure you have a list of options.
✓ Consider what is best for you.
✓ Balance the advantages, thinking of reasons why your choice is good for the other party.
✓ Decide which alternative suggestion might act as a 'stalking horse' and switch attention back where you want it.

4 | TESTING WHERE YOU'VE GOT TO

'Don't assume your opponent agrees with what has been decided so far.'

Everybody has a personal interpretation of situations and events. Three witnesses to the same road traffic accident, for instance, often produce what appear to be three completely different accounts of the same situation. The same is true in negotiations, particularly with regard to details. It is vital, therefore, that you understand as much as possible about your opponent's viewpoint, and that you do not make hasty assumptions about their idea of what has been agreed so far.

Learn to understand the other person's mental map

We all create our own mental maps; a key skill of the effective negotiator is to learn to understand the other side's map. Native Americans have a phrase about walking a mile in the other person's moccasins, and the effective negotiator can learn a lot from this idea.

There are three perspectives you can take on a negotiation situation:

- Your viewpoint;
- Your opponent's viewpoint;
- The 'fly on the wall's' viewpoint.

Under pressure, most people tend to lock themselves into one way of viewing a situation – their viewpoint. As the pressure to complete a negotiation increases with time, this tendency increases. What you should do is to review regularly the other two viewpoints. Imagine what it would be like to be in the other person's position, negotiating against you. What thoughts would be going through their mind? And then the 'fly on the wall's' viewpoint. What would an external, objective observer be noticing in the situation?

Gathering information

You should review a number of issues from all three viewpoints. Firstly, what are the facts of the situation? Ask specific questions of your opponent, to check that your understanding of the facts agrees with theirs. Secondly, there are the feelings involved on both sides. Is frustration creeping into the situation? What are your general feelings about the way the negotiations are progressing? How do you do think the other side is feeling at this stage? Assess the positive aspects of the situation from your viewpoint and check out the other side's reaction to these issues. What do you see as the negative aspects of the situation and, again, bounce these off the other side, with some open questions.

What are you actually doing?

By taking this 'multiple perspective' approach, you are both gathering information and building rapport with your opponent, to establish the common ground. People tend to like people who are like themselves and this process will definitely promote good relations in the negotiation. Be careful that you always retain your distance, though, using the 'fly on the wall's' viewpoint, to avoid becoming too generous in terms of what you are prepared to concede to the other side.

The way it works
Peter, the purchasing manager for a light engineering company, was asked by the managing director to order six new computers from the supplier who could offer the best all-round deal, based on purchase price and warranty terms. After contacting several local suppliers, Peter finally came up with a deal that was much better than all the rest and entered into negotiations towards the final delivery. Although he was not a computer expert, he did understand the basics of the desktop computer, particularly the aspect of random access memory (RAM) and disc storage-capacity, which were both significant issues in the system's specification. As the talks progressed, Peter was focusing more and more on storage and memory capacity and the final deal was struck.

Then the person with whom Peter had been dealing at the computer supplier went on holiday for two weeks, during which the delivery would be taking place. Peter assumed that the supplier had briefed his deputy, who would be finalising the deal about the storage capability of the machines to be supplied. Imagine his embarrassment when, instead of six machines with the required storage at each widely separated workstation, six machines with the lowest specification arrived together, with a centralised, networked tape storage system, for which there was no convenient installation space in the factory. The cost of the cabling and ducting would have been enormous, so the entire shipment had to be returned with consequent loss of use for several weeks. All because Peter did not check that the supplier really understood the details of the specification and how the equipment was to be sited in the factory.

CHECKLIST FOR GETTING IT RIGHT

✓ Review the situation from your viewpoint, in terms of facts and feelings; positives and negatives.

✓ Imagine how the other side thinks about these issues and test the situation with some open questions: for example, what, where, when and how questions.

✓ Imagine you are a 'fly on the wall' – what facts do you need to check, to ensure that both sides are in agreement?

✓ Check the details. It is easy to get carried away with the bigger picture so that the details become assumptions.

✓ Remember the effective use of open questions is vitally important in testing where you have reached in terms of understanding.

'Look for their Achilles' Heel.'

There are times in every negotiation when it is essential to find your opponent's Achilles' Heel, in terms of their style, argument and/or positioning.

This is what to do Before the negotiation, list the factors that are relevant and then prepare the questions that will enable you to find the information you need for you to make wise decisions. Obtaining information from the other side in each of the following areas will enable you to establish their areas of strength and weakness. Any hesitation in answering your questions may indicate concern that your opponent may not be able to live up to the promises made. Those factors are:

1. The Price What do you already know, or can you find out, about their pricing structure and policy?

Question: If we were prepared to place an order for 5,000 items, what would be the discount structure?

2. Delivery Terms Check their current delivery terms and policy. Check if the supplying company uses their own transport or outside contractors.

Question: What are the problems you have experienced with your transport arrangements this year?

3. Quantity Give thought to placing an order for several years' supply, if you able to obtain the right price, delivery and payment terms.

Question: If we were to place a contract order for, say, three years, valued at £500,000, what percentage of your turnover would this represent?

4. Payment Terms Obtain a copy of the other party's accounts and check the ratio between their turnover and debtors. If the debtors list is too large compared to turnover, they will need to negotiate with you for faster payment than normal. You may be prepared to trade this point for special prices, special delivery or any other factor that will suit your arrangements. This is an Achilles' Heel often missed in negotiations. As with all successful negotiations, planning is the key.

5. Financing In the purchase of a major item, the supplying company may offer financing arrangements with a tame or in-house finance company. It is not unusual for a supplying company to receive a commission from the finance house. There are also additional advantages for the supplier in using these finance arrangements, such as quicker payment, staged payments and guaranteed payment. If they attract certain volumes of business to the finance house, they may earn a retrospective discount in rates or a bonus commission.

Solution: Check with the finance house to establish how they deal with the potential suppliers and if commissions or bonuses are available. If they are, you know that you can press hard for a low price, because the supplier will regain any loss in commission, if the purchase is made with the help of their financing company. Having obtained the best price, you should be able to arrange your own finance.

6. Competitors Suppliers new to a market may simply be trying to obtain market-share, sometimes at the expense of profits, in the early years. A typical example of this would be Japanese car-makers. Yes, profits were made in the early years of market penetration; however, prices soon rose when market-share was established. If your supplier is after market-share, their prices will be more flexible than when their market-share is established.

Question: What is your current market-share? To what level do you anticipate taking that share in, say, the next three years?

The use of silence

When you have asked an open question (a question requiring more than a single word or short burst of information as an answer), wait ! Use the power of silence to prompt the other party to continue giving information. Within this further information may be their Achilles' Heel. Too often negotiators not being willing to wait don't gain all the facts they need.

To prompt further information, when your opponent has, apparently, finished speaking, simply say "... and?" and put out your right hand about six inches from your navel, palm up. This enquiring 'hand' and enquiring 'and' will invariably prompt the other person to continue speaking.

CHECKLIST FOR GETTING IT RIGHT

✓ List the factors of the negotiation.
✓ Undertake planning of each and every factor.
✓ Prepare the questions you will ask.
✓ Use the enquiring 'hand' and 'and'.

'Don't fall for the fake stalemate.'

This is a tactic that can be used against you, in an attempt to get you to shift your position and concede an extra point. The better you are at spotting and dealing with this tactic, the more negotiations you will bring to a satisfactory conclusion and the more profitable they will be.

Their comfort stage may not be the same as yours

During the course of negotiations, in amongst the offers, counter-offers, concessions and conditional agreements, there will usually come a time when the other party has reached the 'comfort stage'. This is where they, ideally, wanted to be, paying the price they wanted to pay. This, however, may not be your ideal point or even a deal that you can go ahead with.

It has to be said, though, that not all people will tell you the truth about where their comfort stage starts and finishes.

Watch out for the fake stalemate

This is when they use the fake stalemate, in an attempt to frighten you into believing that you will have to compromise the deal currently on offer. The untrained negotiator at this point either gives up, thinking that the agreement is unattainable, or, even worse, starts conceding points rapidly, trying to buy business at any cost.

The correct procedure, at this point, is to hold your posture and do not panic or show any emotion; you now need to keep the attention firmly focused on your opponent. When they ask you to come up with suggestions of how to overcome this stalemate, you have to respond quickly. You need to state clearly that the proposal as it stands is unacceptable and then put the ball back into their court, by asking a question: "I'm not sure, what do you suggest we do ...?".

What this will do is give the control away to the other side and force them into making some suggestions. Once they have started offering solutions, the whole negotiation process starts again. You may come across a situation in which the other party realises what you are trying to achieve: a game of verbal tennis will ensue.

Whilst this is taking place, no side is making progress; you are not conceding but you are no nearer to closing the negotiations. This is, therefore, counterproductive for both sides.

Focus their attention on finding a solution

In order to stop this switching of focus, without conceding a point, you need to focus their attention on to finding a solution. Bearing in mind that most of these stalemates are fake, and are just gestures to discover who has the stronger will, it is easier to let the other party believe that they have the greater expertise in negotiations.

Do this by simply asking, very firmly "If there was a way that we could go ahead with this deal, we'd like to, but not at the current price" (or state the point you are sticking on). "How would we do it?" or "What would that way be?".

Is the stalemate fake or real? If the stalemate is a fake one, the other party will generally be waiting to produce a favoured solution. They now have the opportunity to present it to you. If, however, there is still no way forward and no concession is made, you have to decide whether or not you can concede and agree the proposal as it stands.

If you are able (and the circumstances allow), withdrawing from the negotiations and leaving the door open for a future date may be the best option. If this option is taken, it is best to withdraw, leaving the focus on them, to contact you if they come up with a solution.

CHECKLIST FOR GETTING IT RIGHT

✓ Make sure they are not steering you into a fake stalemate.
✓ Don't give up and start conceding points.
✓ Hold your position.
✓ Avoid games of verbal tennis, by focusing attention on to finding a solution.
✓ If all else fails, withdraw from the negotiations, leaving the door open for the opposition to restart them.

2 | QUESTIONS, BLUFFS AND RED HERRINGS

7 | HOW TO CHALLENGE YOUR OPPONENT'S ASSUMPTIONS

'The best way is to dig deeply using simple questions to expose their incorrect thinking.'

Assumptions cause more damage to a negotiation than practically anything else. One side or the other jumps to conclusions, almost always the wrong ones. The difficulty lies in discovering where they came from. With the careful use of 'positioned' questions, you can uncover the roots of the assumption and take corrective action immediately.

The way it works

An example of how things can go wrong was highlighted when Mark Rhodes, operations director of a soft drinks company, needed to challenge an assumption long held by a senior buyer of a major chain of superstores. The assumption was due to past poor performance of Mark's company and the buyer had held it for over two years.

A number of attempts by managers had failed to convince the buyer that all was now different but Mark, being new to the business, felt a fresh face might help the situation. A meeting was arranged. Rather than battle against the long-held assumption, Mark decided to examine it from a different position by ignoring it, for the time being, and presenting to the buyer the following questions:

1. "If you knew something was so wrong in your business it was affecting your ability to service your customers properly, you would do everything in your power to correct it, wouldn't you?" Yes, came the reply.

2. "In the past, our business had suffered some difficulties with supply, as many expanding businesses have. That does not excuse us from our duty to you as a preferred account, of course. Things have changed, considerably. My question to you is: what exactly is it that we have to do in order to re-open the account?"

This immediately stopped the buyer from thinking in the past and made them focus on the future. Mark had nothing to lose and everything to gain. The client did open up a small opportunity to supply into six stores for three months; since then, they have agreed once more to go nationwide.

Avoid the politics

Start by not getting caught up in the politics of the situation. Step back into an objective observer's position and consider the options available to you. This may mean a delay in some cases, but it's worth it if you're able to correct wrong assumptions and get your negotiations back on track.

Questions, questions, questions!

The frustrating part is getting started: once you're on your way, the rest is relatively easy. It is advisable to begin with a question that will get the other side to open up about the thinking behind their assumption. If you

15

know the assumption is totally wrong, you must confront the other side with a direct question about why they've drawn this conclusion. An example may well be something like "Alex, you've just said that employing Maria to do that job would be a mistake, as she doesn't have the right experience. Tell me, please, on what basis have you drawn that conclusion?"

Dig deep!   Now you're going to get all the reasons why Alex has come up with his statement. Keep digging. The best way to do this is with simple questions that begin with

- what?
- why?
- when?
- how?
- where?
- who?

You may find some resistance to this; don't be put off. If you want to clear up any misunderstandings, you have to go through this process. Once it is sorted, and the air is cleared, both parties can get back to the business of negotiating and conclude the deal.

CHECKLIST FOR GETTING IT RIGHT

✓ Keep your eye on the main issue; you must uncover where the assumption comes from.
✓ Make your questions expose the other side's thoughts and feelings.
✓ Phrase questions to evoke an open response.
✓ Be sure you get an answer to the question you've asked, before you move on.
✓ Avoid partial answers; get the full picture.
✓ If all else fails, suggest that an independent person helps identify a solution.
✓ Put it in writing: your questions and the response you are looking for.

'answer them confidently ... keep your answers short and authoritative.'

The use and skill of questioning is a major part of any negotiation. By questioning the other party, you obtain information and, at the same time, control the pace and direction of the negotiation. The difficulty comes if you are being asked loaded questions that, whichever way you answer them, might weaken your own position or give away information which is commercially sensitive. The options open to you are:

Ask a question
The first line of defence is to ask a question in return. This is particularly useful early on in the discussion. Do not make any reply to or comment about the question but wait for them to respond to a similarly pointed question of your own. They may answer it or they may decide to drop their approach and try a different angle. Often, loaded questions are used to 'test' you out as a negotiator, particularly in the early stages of the negotiation.

Decline to answer the question
This may sound as if you are admitting a weakness but, if you link this negative reply with an indisputable fact, it is often sufficient to buy you time to move on with a question of your own. The important thing to remember, when using this approach, is to link your reply to something that has already been discussed. Normally, this response works well when the negotiations are well underway.

Question the question
This approach can be very effective if it's done without too much aggression. Getting the tone of the reply right is critical. In effect, you are dismissing the question, by suggesting that there was no real value in asking it.

Agree to come back to it
Acknowledge the question and agree to answer it later on in the discussions, once other matters have been dealt with.

Answer it
By far the most powerful response to a loaded question is to answer it confidently and in a way that implies that you are quite comfortable playing these games, if that is what the other party wants. Keep your answer short and authoritative.

The way it works
James Williams is the regional manager for a genetics company, selling genetically improved animal material around the world to major international businesses working in the food-production and retailing industries. Before deciding to purchase from James' business, these companies like to find out as much as they can about the company, its operations in other countries, and its genetic secrets. Trade in animal products is strictly controlled by intergovernmental agreements.

"Often, I am asked who else I am talking to in the market. This is a loaded question for two reasons. Firstly, they probably know already, as the

17

market for these products in most countries is controlled by a few players, and secondly, if I tell them, it suggests that I shall also tell other companies about my discussions with them. I normally explain that I am talking to several other parties (even if I'm not) and that I am sure that they would not wish me to discuss *their* business with *their* competitors. I then take a more active approach and ask them who their competitors are.

Precedents can be dangerous

"Sometimes, I am asked to include extra tests, beyond those agreed at inter-governmental level. This is also a dangerous situation because, if I agree to these extra tests, I am setting a precedent which will then be in place for as long as the contract exists. If I decline, it suggests that I have something to hide. This will have serious cost implications and will also make it extremely difficult to guarantee continuous product-quality at the new test levels, simply because one is dealing with a biological product. I handle this question by refusing to agree to the request and referring the other party back to their own government's agreed regulations. If their government has agreed to one level of testing, surely that is good enough for them?

"I remember once being asked why the parent company was registered in the Cayman Islands. I answered it by saying that, as I wasn't the owner of the business, I couldn't tell them."

At the end of the day, James knows that these companies wouldn't be talking to him if they didn't need the products his company produces.

CHECKLIST FOR GETTING IT RIGHT

✓ Be aware that you will be asked loaded questions.
✓ Deal with them confidently, as if you are used to dealing with them all the time.
✓ Keep your answers short and based on the minimum number of facts sufficient to answer the question

QUESTION THE WORLD IN WHICH YOUR OPPONENT LIVES

'Ask yourself what you would look for, or accept, if you were in their shoes.'

The way it works

Peter Marchant is managing director of a medium-sized manufacturing company, which prides itself on the good relations between management and staff. But this doesn't come about by accident. It takes understanding and the ability to negotiate the best working deals on both sides.

Peter's staff don't belong to a union or particularly take notice of any workers' rule book. But they do have elected representatives who negotiate pay agreements and working hours and conditions with top management.

"I don't believe in trying to drive the kind of bargain that makes everyone feel resentful and disinclined to work", says Peter, "but I still have a responsibility to company shareholders and I know I can't just award pay rises or extended holidays whenever I would like to. So I put a lot of time and effort before any negotiations take place into finding out what people want – and, more to the point, what they need to maintain their standard of living. Then I can work out how close to that ideal I can come with my final offer.

Find out what they really want

"You see, it's not always about money. A while ago, I realised there was a problem with people asking for afternoons off or coming in late in the mornings. So I asked questions, fairly casually, and found out the local school had changed its times and those with young children were held up getting into work. Some said there was no time to make personal 'phone calls, keep hair or medical appointments or go to their children's school plays, because of our working hours. So this year, when we were sitting down to thrash out the pay agreements, I threw in the idea of flexi-hours as part of the deal. I knew I couldn't match their demands in terms of cash. So I was counting on this tipping the balance.

Be fair

"Of course, I worked out what a fair increase would be before I started. I knew most of them had mortgages and cars to run – there's no point offering something that's so impossible they can't accept. That's just wasting everybody's time. But looking at it from their point of view, I figured a small percentage increase across the board, plus the advantages of the flexi-hour system would make them feel the company recognises their efforts and loyalty – and it makes life easier by allowing them hassle-free time off during the day. It worked marvellously and everybody's happy – except perhaps my secretary, who has to keep a log of the hours everyone works!"

Work it out beforehand

Before you go into a negotiation, it pays to think about what the other side wants out of the deal. In Peter's example, it was fairly clear his staff wanted more money, but, knowing he couldn't meet those demands, he found another viewpoint. He was able to offer a different kind of advantage.

19

This works in all negotiations – because people rarely want money or goods alone. There may also be any number of non-financial reasons why they want those things, such as comfort, security or prestige. Try to find out a bit about your opponent before you start making any deals. Try to anticipate what they really want from you – and why they're negotiating at all. Once you do this, you can have attractive alternatives ready when you go into your meeting.

Ask questions   Don't be afraid to ask questions. If it's another company, 'phone up and ask what they do. Get their brochure, ask for their price lists. It's the only way you'll find out how they think. When you're dealing with an individual, take time for some casual conversation before your negotiations begin – even if it's only on the phone. Ask how their family is and where they come from – any information of this kind can be revealing.

Then ask yourself why these people are doing business with you. What do they want from you? Is it because your product is the best on the market – or the cheapest? Is it because you can deliver quickly and efficiently? If it's a salary negotiation, as in the example, why are you negotiating? Are they demanding more than you think reasonable? If so, is there a reason why? Are working conditions hazardous – or longer than average? What would you consider reasonable in their shoes to do what they do?

CHECKLIST FOR GETTING IT RIGHT

✓ Find out what kind of person you are dealing with.
✓ Ask questions to find out what this person or company really wants from you.
✓ Decide what alternatives you can offer them and have your alternative options ready.
✓ Be reasonable! If they have grounds for more negotiation, consider them.

10 | WHAT TO DO WHEN YOUR BLUFF IS CALLED

'Don't bluff unless you can take it all the way to the wire.'

There is an old gag which tells of the motorist who asked a pedestrian the way to somewhere. He is told, "I wouldn't have started from here".

Watch this health warning

The point is, that you should not bluff in the first place, unless you are prepared to have your bluff called. Bluffing is a game to be played only by those who know it, enjoy it, and are prepared for the eventuality of being 'called'. The highways and byways of negotiation-land are strewn with the bodies of those who gave it a faint-hearted try ... and lost. So, before we go any further into this subject, it is worth issuing a stern health-warning: don't bluff unless you are prepared to take it all the way to the wire.

However, if you are of an adventurous disposition, relish the psychological cut-and-thrust of the poker game and are not easily fazed, bluffing is one of the most powerful weapons that you can include in your negotiation armoury.

The drawback of calling a bluff

What is a bluff? Let us examine its nature, and its weaknesses.

A bluff is a lie. It is an untruth that is uttered or implied in order to deceive the opposition into believing that your position is stronger than it actually is. So far, so good; like any lie, a bluff has the potential weakness of needing to be backed up. You may be able to spin a glib and plausible story that has the opposition on the run, for example, telling them all about the other people who are desperate to grab this opportunity if they aren't interested, but what if they suddenly turn and call you?

Inveterate bluffers know that this rarely happens in a straightforward, confrontational way – people seldom call other people liars – which is one of the strengths of the bluff. But, if you are in with another bluffer, if your opposition also enjoys the game and is sharp-witted enough, they can turn the game around and 'hoist you with your own petard'.

The way it works

Joshua Ravenscroft enjoys wheeler-dealing. He's been doing it since he was a teenager with a market stall. Today he deals in paper; not just a few packets of stationery, but lorry-loads of paper in bulk.

"But paper isn't my business, really. I tell people I'm in the transport business, which really is true. Paper is dirt-cheap at cost and at the depot, but it's very heavy. So nearly all the cost is in getting it to the customer. That's why I say I'm in transport.

"When I started in the business, there were still mugs who would buy paper ex-depot and think they were getting a hell of a bargain till they got the bill and saw what the transport had cost them – but that's another story.

21

"I'd been trying for ages to get a contract, supplying newsprint to a local newspaper up north, and I'd been getting nowhere. So, one day, I started trying to impress them by boasting about all the people I was supplying. I was trotting out all these names – some of them true – including some other businesses in the north. I'd made sure that none of them advertised in the newspaper, so it'd be more difficult for them to check – not that anyone ever bothers to check – but he turns round and says that, if I'm already delivering up there, I could consolidate the loads and reduce delivery charges.

"It was the last thing I expected! I was actually trying to break into the north. There was no one else. I'd thought he'd be a good starter. I should have known that a newspaper would be good at buying paper. Anyway, I had to think pretty quick.

"I told him that the others were buying complete loads, so there was no spare on my permitted axle weight, but I was thinking of opening a northern depot. Then I left pretty fast.

"The funny thing was that, months later, I did break into the north – but not through them – and did open a northern depot. That's when I got their contract. Have I bluffed him since? I'm not saying – he may read this. But I gained much more respect for northern know-how through him."

CHECKLIST FOR GETTING IT RIGHT

- ✓ What to do when your bluff is called? Every bluff is different, so there is no one answer. If you need to ask, you should not be bluffing in the first place.
- ✓ How to call a bluff? You do not need bluntly to accuse the bluffer of lying. Make a suggestion or request that can be viable only if what they are saying is true.

11 PRETENDING YOU'VE MISUNDERSTOOD THE POSITION

'Use it to steer the negotiation your way.'

In a situation where you have reached a stalemate and the position of the deal is strongly in your favour, the opposition may believe that they are fighting a lost cause and give up. In this case, you need to offer them a glimmer of hope. Pretending that you have misunderstood a point, and that conceding it, can encourage them to begin thinking positively again and allows the negotiations to continue.

A pause for reflection can be beneficial

There are also times during negotiations where things are proceeding at a quicker pace than you wish; maybe too many points have been conceded and a pause for reflection would be beneficial. Claiming again that you have misunderstood one or all of the points, and asking for clarification, allows you to take time and, if need be, lets you retract a point previously conceded.

In either case, the main objective is to be able to re-evaluate the situation, without giving the appearance of changing your mind or losing face. You will, however, have to offer to take the responsibility for the misunderstanding; the other party may feel that they did not make themselves clear, however, and offer an apology. It is only fair to assure them that this is unimportant, to put them at ease, before you go on to renegotiate the points that you are uncomfortable with.

Obviously, this tactic has to be adapted to the particular situation that you have arrived at in the negotiations, but, as a general rule, call a halt to proceedings by saying "I am sorry, Mr Applegate, but we have covered so many points and there are so many variations that I am a little confused. Can we go over the points again, because I believe that we may have different ideas as to the agreement so far?".

Let them take the floor

This allows Mr Applegate to take the floor. While you sit back and listen, he proceeds to give you his version of the points agreed so far. Then, when he reaches the specific area you wish to change, interrupt by saying "I am sorry that I led you to believe that we had agreed that point and the misunderstanding is my fault. I believed that my agreeing that point was subject to ...". Or, "I thought that I agreed that point in addition to the other part of the negotiation and not instead of". This then allows you to offer the solution and take blame for the confusion by saying "Can I make a suggestion? As I have clearly complicated the proceedings by not being able to keep track of events, can we start again? But as we agree points I will write them down so we both fully understand what it is we are agreeing to. Would that be all right with you?".

Use the time bought to plan your response

This tactic will allow you enough time to fully understand the agreement on offer and to plan any responses or arguments, to help you close the negotiations at a satisfactory point.

Claiming that you have misunderstood a point, or the whole of the negotiations, can also be used as a tactic to get the other side to concede points. If there is another process to complete after the negotiations, for example, board approval or another party's, then you can claim that you misunderstood and reported the agreement (with the misunderstanding) to that party. The misunderstanding may be only a minor point, such as delivery charges and times, or inclusive or exclusive of V.A.T., and, although you take responsibility, it will be another period of time, with a lot more trouble to get the agreement re-accepted. You can also ask that it be a personal favour to you that this point is conceded, as this situation would obviously embarrass you to your peers.

CHECKLIST FOR GETTING IT RIGHT

✓ Pretending that you have misunderstood a point and then conceding encourages a negotiator who is about to give up think positively again.

✓ Four uses for a misunderstanding:

- It can slow the proceedings down, when the negotiations are going too fast for you.
- It can be used to retract a point you had conceded, without you losing face.
- You can buy yourself time to plan your response.
- You can use it to gain a concession.

12 | STATISTICS AND FIGURES THAT ARE USED TO BLIND, BLUFF AND JUSTIFY

'... I must be sure exactly what you are saying before I can respond ...'

Negotiation is often about numbers: figures, statistics, percentages and perhaps several permutations of each. It may well be here that the heart of any agreement that needs to be thrashed out lies; indeed, there may be significant profit, or savings, hanging on the outcome.

At the same time, numerical complexity provides an opportunity for a skilled negotiator to confuse and gain an edge based on the other party's sheer inability to handle the figures, or at least to do so sufficiently fast.

Let us be honest: not everyone has the same degree of numeracy (something you might want to improve?). There is even an old tale of a statistician who drowned wading across a river with an average depth of three feet! And a true story of a buyer running rings around a sales person, until the seller notices that the calculator which the buyer keeps using, and from which they make detailed financial claims: "That's only 0.5 per cent better than the other offer I have", is not actually switched on. Clearly, an area in which to beware of bluffs.

So there is a need here for some circumspection. Preparation is again, not surprisingly, key. You will be far more likely to be caught out or put on the spot if you do not put yourself in a position to check numbers that are quoted at you. So, work out the permutations in advance. For example, if you are negotiating a price which necessitates conversion to a foreign currency, it may be useful not only to have a note of exchange rates, but also a simple list of various benchmark figures, ready-converted for instant reference.

Particular hazards

It is worth considering those things that might be – perhaps intentionally – used to confuse; given particular circumstances, some factors may not be difficult to anticipate. For example:

- The scale chosen for a graph can easily be designed to emphasise one factor rather than another, or to minimise one aspect of what it demonstrates.

- Exactitude may not mean what it seems: a figure may be quoted to three decimal places, but still be an estimate.

- Something printed out from a computer may seem to possess gospel certainty, but contain a number taken off the nearest bus.

A key ploy of which to beware is time, or rather lack of it. Someone may attempt to railroad an agreement through by rattling off figures, allowing no consideration or query; the classic 'blinding with science' technique.

25

Slow the pace   Given suitable preparation, the most useful response is to slow the pace and make sure – absolutely sure – that you appreciate the full significance of any figures being used by the other side, and are thus able to respond to them suitably and from the basis of fact.

The way it works   Many situations involve not only figures, but the interrelation of a number of different factors. Anthony Bird is concerned with the international distribution arrangements for his company's range of machine tools. There are many variables here that involve figures: price, delivery, service arrangements, margins, spare parts, etc.; today, he is having trouble with the Malaysian distributor, who persistently throws out figures to support his case, especially a plethora of percentages. Anthony is experienced and reasonably well prepared. He needs time to assess what is really going on. He interrupts, while acknowledging the importance of what the other person is saying: "Hold on – this is getting somewhat complicated. I must be sure of exactly what you are saying before I can respond properly. Perhaps I can recap". Pause. "Let's see". Pause. "If I understand rightly, there are three issues here: the overall discounts, the payment terms and the effect of any currency changes. Now what you are saying is, first, that discounts ...".

Given the complexity, his need to recap is surely unarguable. He reorganises the barrage of figures into three sections and summarises to clarify the position (and give time for thought – proceeding at a pace that makes it clear he, in fact, insists on thinking it through).

This allows a considered response. What is more, if this sort of recap makes it clear that a bluff was intended, it may throw more power on to his side as the conversation continues: "It seems to me your initial point here missed a key issue: what we really have to consider is ... ". In such a way, figures introduced with an element of confusion can be aired again – and the real facts dealt with – and the likelihood of any further bluff reduced.

CHECKLIST FOR GETTING IT RIGHT

✓ Make absolutely sure you do your homework.
✓ Have any necessary notes or references with you.
✓ Do not allow yourself to be rushed.
✓ Get the facts straight in your mind.
✓ Insist on time to deal with the real issues.
✓ Use any evidence of bluff to suggest deviousness that may warrant a compensating concession.

13 | FLUSH OUT THE LIES

'Ask questions all the time.'

Don't assume that everyone you negotiate with is as honest as you are. Be on the lookout for those little bends in the truth – and the downright lies that some negotiators think they can get away with. "It's company policy" is one of them. "There's only this much left in the budget" is often another. All right, you're not certain it's a lie. You don't have to accuse anyone – but you don't have to accept what's said at face value, either.

Have your questions ready

Ask questions all the time. Ask when the company policy was formulated – by whom. In what other instances was it used? Ask when the company budgets are set. When would the next allocation be made? What provisions are made for your kind of product or proposal? The more details you demand, the more difficult it is for the other side to uphold false statements.

If your opponent passes the buck, ask to speak to the person who makes the decisions. If they refuse, request that they get clarification from that person. There's no point in trying to strike a deal with someone who hasn't got the authority to agree it. Suggest you call a coffee break while they do it or postpone the negotiations until you're both clear on what can or can't be done.

And, if they're selling goods to you, ask why the price is set as it is. What is included for that amount and what are the alternatives. If you get a chance, check with competitors to see if the information you're getting is comparable.

Don't be blinded by science

Sometimes the lie isn't so easy to spot. The other side might try to blind you with science. If this happens, and you suspect they're trying to fool you, make a joke of your terrible head for figures or your total inability with computers. There are two alternatives here – either ask for time to take the figures away with you and look them over, or insist you call in an expert. Both ways give you a chance to get another, independent view of the information and buy time for you to think over the implications.

The way it works

Julian Tapley learned this lesson the hard way. His printing works spent out thousands of pounds on computerised equipment and software that wasn't necessary and didn't do the job he expected. And there was nothing he could do about it, because he entered into the deal without checking the technical facts and figures involved. "After that experience, I'm constantly on my guard", says Julian. "If someone wants to negotiate a deal with me, I make sure I understand every little detail – right down to who's signing the contract and whether I get a chance to change my mind."

Listen and take notes

"As soon as someone starts laying down ground rules, I'm listening very carefully. I even take notes. Then I can go back to the subject afterwards and ask more questions without interrupting the flow of the conversation at the time. In fact, it's sometimes more effective to throw in a casual question later on, when they've forgotten what they said. If I get a different answer, I say something like: 'Oh, I must have misunderstood earlier – didn't you say...' It works every time and puts them off their stride.

"Of course, I lose a deal sometimes. People don't always like being questioned. But I feel that someone who's genuine and really wants to come to a win-win agreement with me, would be comfortable with my questions. If they're trying to cheat me now, at this early stage, what else might they do later on?"

CHECKLIST FOR GETTING IT RIGHT

✓ Probe for more details.
✓ Question 'blanket' statements that close off options completely.
✓ Take notes.
✓ Ask who made policy decisions your opponent says are immutable and demand to speak to the person concerned.
✓ If they try to 'blind you with science', play for more time, to allow you to grasp the details.
✓ Call in the experts to explain difficulties to you.

3 | SUBTLE SMOKESCREENS AND TRICKY TRADES

'Don't over-react, but stay cool and in control.'

So there you are, confidently closing the deal and, at the last minute, they drop a bombshell. They might tell you that:

- Due to circumstances beyond their control, the required specification of the product has altered significantly enough to increase your costs, but the budget has not.
- Another department has overspent their budget, so now your customer has less money to spend.
- Someone else has entered the game with a similar product at a lower price.

The first question to be addressed is whether you believe it. It could be a bluff. But is it?

Make some constructive guesses

You may think that there is no surefire answer to this, and that is true, up to a point. But constructive guessing, based on what you already know (and what you know is that the timing is crucially bad for you) can help you formulate a suitable response.

So why now? Isn't it suspicious that this news arrived at the most inconvenient time for you? A week earlier, you were still discussing the price, specification and so on, and this new factor would have been central to the negotiations. Now you have already begun committing yourself to the necessary courses of action to process the business (they were the ones who were urging top priority), in good faith, based on what had already been agreed. A bluff is looking likely.

This is not to say that they have invented the story. They might have simply held up telling you about it till the last possible moment, in order to give themselves an edge. But that is still a form of bluff. The first piece of advice here is not to believe in accidents (particularly accidents that are unhappy for you).

So what do you do?

Don't bluntly call their bluff

Bluntly calling a bluff is the last thing you should do. This is not to say that it is never an advisable course of action, simply that other courses should be tried first. A straight 'call' is tantamount to accusing the opposition of lying, and that has serious repercussions on the relationship you have been working towards building. Also, there could be very good reasons (from their perspective) for the bluff.

The way it works

Let's see what Mary Chatteris did in such circumstances. She has her own head-hunting consultancy and was working with a prospective client company, to prepare a proposed campaign to find them a new operations director. As part of her proposal, she had needed to get costings on advertising space in certain national newspapers; in order to get those newspapers to commit to favourable (and toughly negotiated) prices, she had made at least moral commitments, on her own part, to buy that space.

At the eleventh hour, the prospective client started bringing up problems. The budget that they had suggested was suddenly cut back. Unless she took a swingeing cut in her own profit, some of that advertising space was now out of the question. If she simply cancelled it, she would lose, with those newspapers, credibility that she had painstakingly built up over a sustained period. And the most galling part of her dilemma was a deeply-held conviction that it was all a try-on anyway.

Turn a dilemma to your advantage

"But I didn't accuse them of trying it on. Nor did I bang the table and rant about my problems. I simply laid out my initial proposal against a rapidly-revised one that was based on the new budget figures. I explained how the scaled-down campaign was going to be radically less effective, homing in particularly on the drastically reduced percentage chances of their finding the right person for this crucial position. It was pretty dramatic to see how quickly they put the budget back where it was.

"If my proposal and its costings had been flawed, or over-inflated, their try-on would have exposed me (which is probably why they did it). But I know my job, and I do my costings conscientiously, honestly and well. By simply going on doing my job, I exposed them rather than they me."

CHECKLIST FOR GETTING IT RIGHT

✓ Realise that although you are probably faced with a bluff, there may be good reasons for it.
✓ Realise that, this being the case, you have nothing to fear if you are being honest.
✓ Don't over-react, but stay cool and in control of the situation.
✓ By appearing to go along with the new circumstances, expose the disadvantages to them of changing the deal.

15 | USING A SMOKESCREEN

'The associate's document had been a complete red herring.'

Planning your negotiation is critical; there are too many examples of negotiations that have failed as a result of lack of planning. One element of the planning phase is to decide what is important for you to have, and what you can give away in order to get it. Having decided this, you may need to plan the best way of ensuring you get what you want. The order in which you discuss the issues can be critical. It is here that a smokescreen may be helpful, to conceal your intentions.

The running order

Several issues may be linked together and, until you have uncovered all of them, you do not wish to trade. Decide where you want to start the negotiations. Often, by choosing an issue which is relatively unimportant to you, but making it sound as if it is central to your needs, you can identify a number of areas in the other person's proposals where you might be able to achieve a positive outcome.

Where there's a choice

Try and create situations within the negotiation where there is a choice of options available to you. Identify the outcome that is most favourable to you, but emphasise the others. This needs to be done carefully, because you do not want to end up with this option. Overplayed, it is easy to spot, and an experienced negotiator will see your tactic for what it is. Try to get the other party to move or to express intransigence. If they move, push a little more strongly for further compromise. As soon as they show resistance, suggest looking at other options (including the one you want). If they show intransigence, ask them to make a suggestion. They will almost certainly suggest another of the options.

Trading back a concession

This entails gaining a concession that you may then be able to trade back for the concession you really want. You are offered extra holiday as part of a new salary package. You take it, but really want a better basic salary. You trade the holiday entitlement back later in the negotiations, in order to get the basic salary rate up.

The red herring

This should only be used when other, more direct, approaches are closed to you. It is only recommended for situations in which the stance of the other party is one of non co-operation, or you need them to move quite a way from their opening position.

A few years ago, a team of associate consultants was asked to discuss new contract terms with the organisation for which they worked. The organisation was in the public sector and the management team had been

The terms were very unfavourable

asked to reduce costs. Associate consultants' fees and expenses were seen as one area where reductions could be implemented. The associates discovered that the management team were going to present a *fait accompli* at the meeting to negotiate the new arrangements. The terms that had been drawn up were very unfavourable to the associates. The associates prepared another document with terms as unfavourable to the management side as the management team's were to theirs. Soon after the meeting had started, and the management team's proposal had been put forward, the associates presented theirs. It included all sorts of demands that they had no intention of pushing for. The management team was furious and threatened to walk out of the meeting. The associates replied that the management's approach had made them feel the same way.

After some further discussion, both parties agreed to chuck their documents in the bin and start afresh. They ended up with a much more positive outcome for both parties. The associates' document had been a compete red herring: a smokescreen, designed to hide the real needs of the associates while forcing flexibility into the management team's position.

CHECKLIST FOR GETTING IT RIGHT

✓ If you think the opposition is putting up a smokescreen, probe it, by asking questions.

✓ Don't necessarily start with your main demand; start with an issue which will help you to uncover all the key points.

✓ Don't be too quick to get into detail.

16 | POWER IS ONLY A PERCEPTION

'Power, like beauty, is in the eye of the beholder.'

In all walks of life, the perception of power comes into play and misperceptions abound. Just think how many times we make assumptions about others, how many times we make assumptions about situations and how many times we judge the book by the cover. Some years ago, I was fortunate to have the use of a chauffeur. This lasted for five years. During that period I learnt that power really is a perception.

So many occasions when, having arrived at a client's office by chauffeur-driven car, I was met with a deference unbecoming for the situation or my perception of myself. It was one of the most instructive experiences of my life.

What can we learn from those experiences? Well ... if you have a particularly important meeting or negotiation to go to, hire a car with a chauffeur: you will be amazed at the difference it will make, both to the other party and yourself. So, if perception is more important than reality (and it is!), part of the planning at the start of any negotiation or persuasion must be the question "How do I wish to be perceived ?".

Consider the following :

1. Dress
We tend to believe people in authority or those we perceive as experts in their field. We make these perceptions, very often, by the way in which the person is dressed. If the outcome of the negotiation justifies the expense, invest in the appropriate wardrobe, fitting to the occasion. An expensive business suit with matching shirt or blouse, accompanied by scarf or tie, will set the scene before you even utter the first word.

2. Car
Whilst perhaps most of us would like to hold to the idea that a person's car does not make a difference to how they are perceived, we also know that in today's materialistic world, a car's make, model, colour and registration plate always makes a statement about its owner. Hiring or renting a prestigious car, just for the day or week, is often money well spent.

3. Accessories
We have all heard people mention makes of watches, jewellery, ties, socks, shoes and every other accessory imaginable. In the late eighties and early nineties, many people were judged by the accessories they wore or didn't wear. If you believe that the other party to your negotiation might be influenced by the accessories you do or do not wear, use appropriate ones. As with all aspects of negotiation, perception included, nothing should be left to chance; nothing should be done by default.

4. Venue
Surprisingly the venue of the negotiations can have a dramatic effect on the outcome. Rather like framing the outcome of a meeting by stipulating the potential benefits of agreement, the venue pre-frames the discussion. Talks held over a grubby canteen table are far, far different from those

held over the immaculate white table cloth of the best table in a high-class restaurant or tea-rooms. If you wish to put forward a powerful perception, give great thought to the venue. Obviously, a breakfast meeting in Paris at the George V will be perceived as more powerful than a meeting at the local motorway service station.

5. Briefcase   Strange to think that the case in which we carry our papers should have such an effect on other people; however, examine your own perceptions in this area. One person has suggested that people perceive an inverse relation between briefcase size and personal power: the larger the case ... the lower the perceived power. The smaller the briefcase ... the greater the perceived power. Until the ultimate, someone else to carry your case. This seemingly minor point can pre-frame any meeting. I have seen it in play and been amazed at the difference it made.

6. Testimonials   The power of testimonials is used by advertisers, direct-mail companies and salespeople the world over. It is possible to use testimonials in the never-ending power play that takes place in most negotiations. Spoken testimonials can be introduced before the meeting, by having someone to promote you or your product/service to the other party. In some situations, you may be able to arrange for another person to be with you for the negotiations. Before the meeting, arrange and practise with the other person to co-promote each other. I have used this idea and it works extremely well.

Some years ago, a colleague of mine told me about an idea he had read in a book by Clement Freud. This is how it worked. Knowing that I was going to a restaurant for dinner one evening, my friend, just for fun, telephoned the restaurant prior to my arrival and left a message for me "To call the minister's office urgently!" I was amazed at the attitude of the restaurant management to this message. As a regular at the restaurant, I waited six months before disclosing the truth. Try it for yourself and see what happens.

7. Modelling   One easy way to create a perception of power is to model yourself on or reflect how you believe a high-powered person would be. Consider smiling less often, walking more purposefully, standing and sitting more upright. Avoid smoking and drinking. Make a list of your perceptions of powerful attributes and then model that list. After all, power, like beauty, is in the eye of the beholder.

CHECKLIST FOR GETTING IT RIGHT

✓ Perception is power.
✓ Plan everything.
✓ Model powerful people.
✓ Decide how you wish to be perceived.
✓ Question yourself to realise your power.

17 | DEMANDING A CONCESSION

'All the time you are 'spinning plates'. How many can you keep spinning at the same time?'

Concessions are what negotiation is about. If you simply to agree to what is on offer, you may have a quieter life but you are not negotiating. The entire negotiation process is about looking for concessions from the opposition and, if necessary, trading them off against concessions from you. The basic skill involved is twofold:

- You have to be able to persuade them that your demands are reasonable;
- You have to be able to evaluate their offers very quickly.

The trouble with these is that:

- No one can tell you in advance if you are being reasonable;
- No one can do that evaluation for you.

The fair price versus the reasonable demand

Just as there is no fixed formula for establishing a 'fair' price, there is no formula that an outsider can give for what constitutes a reasonable demand. A price becomes fair when the seller has persuaded the buyer that they are getting good value. A demanded concession becomes reasonable when the other side deems it so. An offered counter-concession is a good deal if it has a comparable (or greater) value to you.

A complicated negotiation can be filled with a large number of concessions and trade-off concessions, all forming part of the overall package. And this increases the number of skills you need.

How many different bits of information can you process, evaluate, and hold in your memory? It makes you sound a bit like a computer; but no computer could perform the task like the human brain, because many of the ingredients have little or no market-value in themselves – only some sort of subjective benefit to you. All the time you are 'spinning plates'. How many can you keep spinning at the same time?

Watch out for unnecessary 'plates'

A ploy that is often used by negotiators is to add unnecessary 'plates' for spinning, i.e. overcomplicating the package. The idea is to get the opposition so bogged down in dozens of little trade-offs that they lose sight of the overall picture, which, bit by bit is shifting against them.

Therefore, it is important that you guard against this in various ways:

- **Keep notes.** My most useful piece of high-tech equipment is an A4 pad.
- **Keep cool.** If the negotiation looks as if it is getting into a frenzy, slow the discussion down. How? Ask a question.
- **Step back from the 'canvas'.** An artist painting a picture often goes back to the other side of the room, to look at the picture from a distance.

Guard against your nose being pressed too close to extraneous detail for you to able to see the 'big picture'.

● **Develop an instinct** for spotting 'red-herring' concessions.

Many negotiators have allowed themselves to be led down blind alleys, with lots of little concessions dangled in front of their noses, only to turn around and find that they have given away a disproportionate amount in return.

The way it works

Nick Solway is a chartered surveyor, who specialises in office premises. His working life is constant negotiation. He negotiates to get the business in the first place and then has to negotiate on his client's behalf. Sometimes, he is negotiating to let property; sometimes, to rent it.

"When you are dealing with a lease on something as complicated as office space, concessions are flying around like frisbees. You start from a baseline of square footage, and its going-rate in that location, and go on from there. If all tenants wanted an open square space, and all premises were open squares, I'd be out of a job. Every prospective tenant company has its own requirements in terms of optimum layout: every set of premises has its own idiosyncrasies. So it's always going to be a compromise."

I work towards making the scales balance or tip in my favour

"And in the event of the premises being perfect in every respect for the client's requirements, you invent compromises – because that's where the concessions are. The technique I use is that of visualising a set of scales. Each concession I make goes on one side, and each concession they make goes on the other, and, bit by bit, I am working towards making the scales either balance or tip in my favour. In my early days, I used to list the two sides on a sheet of paper with a value to each concession, on a scale of one to ten, in brackets beside it. By totting up the brackets on each side I saw how I was doing. (Actually I was pretty sneaky! My values to their concessions were coded one-down from what I thought their value actually was and mine were coded one-up. So I could show the opposition my calculations and show them how unreasonable they were being!) I would recommend that as a technique to anyone not used to the process."

CHECKLIST FOR GETTING IT RIGHT

✓ In the process of give and take, make sure you take at least as much as you give.

✓ Don't be led down blind alleys by strings of concessions that turn out to be red herrings.

✓ Step back from the 'canvas': never lose sight of the big picture.

✓ If necessary, tot it all up on paper (coding, if you like).

18 | SPLITTING THE DIFFERENCE

'If the difference is small compared to the size of the concessions, splitting the difference is usually acceptable.'

This is one of the purest forms of negotiations and the most commonly used by people to end an uncomfortable negotiation experience quickly. However, it does have its uses.

What it means when it's used early on

If the 'splitting the difference' tactic is used as an opening gambit, it is usually a sign that the person using it is not comfortable entering into a lengthy negotiation. Their idea is that it is worth asking for some kind of concession, in the hope that they may achieve a slightly better price or improve on the deal just for having the nerve to ask. As this is the most commonly known tactic, if it is used at the beginning of the negotiation, it may be that it is the only tactic known to your opponent; if this is the case, a very short explanation as to why this would be impossible, followed by another request for the order, is usually enough to switch the emphasis back to them and achieve an agreement to go ahead.

When they don't take 'no' for an answer

Very often, this will leave them with "oh well, I tried" and the "if you don't ask, you don't get" feelings and, of course, this means that they were never seriously trying to negotiate with you in the first place. If someone refuses to take no for an answer, and tries to split the difference again, this may be just a testing ploy. If this happens, try to pacify them by offering a very small concession, maybe even one that you were going to give away anyway. This may be a free delivery or something small in comparison to the item subject to the negotiation.

Shut the door to stop conceding more

As always, it is better to agree to give extra product or service as opposed to discounting price and an agreement to go ahead subject to your meeting any concession must be clearly obtained before you actually give anything. You may be able to get this agreement by saying "if I am able to do that ..." or "if I can get this agreed ... then you guarantee to go ahead and place the order now". This obviously closes the door on any further negotiation after that point has been agreed.

This particular ploy does have its uses: after lengthy negotiations, it can be that both parties believe that they have conceded enough and a stalemate arises. This is very often a case of posturing or giving in to peer pressure, rather than a genuine financial issue. In this instance, if the difference is relatively small compared to the size of the concessions made by either party, a request to split the difference is acceptable. However, it has to be stated in such a way as not to let the other party see it as another ploy and dismiss it.

Exaggerate the amount you are conceding

To split the difference successfully, you must focus your opponent's attention on the fact that you are conceding fifty per cent of the difference. You would do this by revisiting the whole agreement so far, emphasising the concessions that you have already made; at this point, the more you can exaggerate the difference between the deal that you wanted in the first instance and the one you have on offer now, the more effectively this tactic will work.

After you have highlighted these differences, focus on the main reason for your wish to go ahead with the agreement and give this as the only reason that you decide to concede yet again. Agree to half of the difference in terms or price, to bring the negotiations to a close. By focusing on the fact that you have conceded fifty per cent of the disputed amount, you allow the other party to maintain their posture and agree with you to close the negotiations.

CHECKLIST FOR GETTING IT RIGHT

✓ If it is used early on, the negotiator probably lacks experience.
✓ If you have to, offer a very small concession.
✓ Exaggerate your concession to make it seem like an equal half.
✓ Close the negotiations by agreeing "if I am able to do this, then you will guarantee to go ahead".

19 | DISTORTING THE VALUE OF AN OFFER

'Always trade something which is of value to the other party but of less value to you ...'

During negotiations, there comes a point when offers are made as a way of trying to close the deal. The person making the offer does so in terms that are favourable to them but in a way that sounds attractive to you. The key to all successful negotiations is listening to what has been said and seeing 'behind' it, to understand the full meaning and what it brings you in real benefit.

Breaking down the offer

For example, a large sum for a capital item is broken down into smaller parts, so that what you think you are getting is a low-cost way of financing the purchase. It hasn't changed the total sum involved. You receive a cost-per-head for the annual company dinner which sounds reasonable but still means that you are going to spend over £1,000 on the night. A £1,000 for one night, to a restaurant, is an enormous amount of money.

If the restaurant tries to break it down into smaller figures, keep building it back up to the total amount. What it will cost you is the total figure when you have finally paid for it, not the price per head or the cost per month.

They offer extras

You negotiate to move into a new office unit with the leasing agents. As part of the deal, they throw in a range of ancillary services 'for nothing' and agree to fix the rent for three years. You think that you have got a good deal but, in fact, many of the ancillary services would cost you very little if you need them at all, and, in the meantime, you are paying a higher rent. Always ask yourself "Do I need these extras and, if I do, can I get them for less money from someone else?".

Keep referring back to the key element, the rent. Ask what the rent would be if they removed all these extras. Ask what rent review would be proposed if the length of time before the first rent review was altered. Always take them back to the heart of the negotiation. You can always buy the extras when you need them.

Remove the 'value' of the extras

They offer extras as part of the deal and tell you how attractive this makes the offer. Tell them that you do not value their offer in the same way.

They offer you terms which include the exclusive use to use their trade name. You tell them that the use of their trade name is of little value to you, because your own name in the market is well known and has a strong reputation.

They offer you longer payment terms if you buy at the prices they propose. You advise them that your cash flow is strong and you don't need longer to pay. What you want is to agree a lower price than they are offering for the goods and services you wish to purchase.

They offer a full technical support service as part of the deal. You tell them that you would expect that anyway, paying the kind of prices they are quoting! They suggest that the offer they are making is very generous, given all the other work that they will be giving you later in the year. Ask yourself "What other work?". "Is it guaranteed?" (it never is!). "What value is the work that I am doing for them now?" and "What other options do I have?".

Their values are not yours   Watch out for comments such as "This is a very fair offer" or "These are standard terms and conditions that the whole industry works to". Their values are simply that – their values. You may think that it is an unreasonable offer. If you do, say so. The whole of the industry may work to these standard terms and conditions (highly unlikely) but you are not the whole industry. Challenge them, if you think that they are not reasonable. Don't allow the other party to influence you by distorting the value of an offer they make.

The way it works   Lynn Saunders is the export administrative manager for her company and regularly books hotel accommodation for the sales team. "I tend to deal with hotels directly if the country is outside Europe. They invariably quote their top rate and then offer a range of extras such as king-size beds, free breakfasts, newspapers, upgrades and such like. All the team is interested in is a comfortable room, within easy distance of our customer's sites and good service.

"I tell the hotels that I want single rooms at their best rate. The only extra that is of value is late check-out, as this can save a half-day room charge. I only ask for this once the rate had been agreed for the reservation. All the other extras I devalue."

CHECKLIST FOR GETTING IT RIGHT

✓ Build up an offer, if the other party is breaking it down.
✓ Watch out for the real value of extras.
✓ If the extras are of no value to you, say so and remove them from the negotiation.

4 BOTTLENECKS AND BODY LANGUAGE

'When we really get talking ... we usually find a new area of agreement.'

Some negotiations speed through easily: there's plenty of room for manoeuvre on both sides and the outcome is satisfactory to everyone. But there are times when the needs of the two sides just can't be reconciled. Either your prices are too high or their demands are beyond your capabilities. If the negotiation goes on, one side will either have to give in and lose out on the deal or you'll have to walk away. No one likes to leave without reaching an agreement, so, if you see this situation coming, it's worth slowing down the negotiation and talking around the situation, until something new occurs to you.

Find something new to add to the equation

What you're looking for is some new piece of information, something extra you can throw into the equation, to make your proposal more attractive or theirs more achievable. It doesn't have to hinge on cost – it could be something to do with the benefits of your service or product. It could even be personal to the manager concerned, rather than the business.

Take a break from formal discussions

Call a halt to the formal discussions. Ask for a coffee break or, better still, adjourn for lunch or dinner. Use this break as an excuse to talk informally to your opposition. Don't rush this stage of the proceedings, you want to get all the background information you can. Ask as many questions as possible. What do you want to achieve? Why do you need to do it this way? What would convince you to change your mind about some of the points?

Then, when you go back to your formal discussions, you can be ready with your amended offer.

How it works

Ben Aldercroft's company specialises in catering and corporate entertainment. He's often involved in negotiations between big entertainment venues and companies wanting something memorable for their delegates.

"It sounds easy, but we often reach a deadlock in our discussions, because the venues want far more in payment for the special events than the companies want to pay. Or the companies demand facilities that we can't provide, because the venue won't allow them. I feel like I'm sandwiched in the middle, trying to come up with the best answer for both sides.

"There are times when it looks as though we just can't agree on anything. The companies want to do business, but they can't see a solution to their differences – they are too far apart in their expectations.

Find out what they really want

"What I do is stop the formal negotiations and ask to contact the venue again at a later date. Then I take the negotiator from the paying company out to lunch, where I can try to get a different, less formal, perspective on the problem. I ask what kind of clients they're entertaining and what sort of impression they want to make on them.

"It sometimes happens that, when we start talking it over, the venue they've chosen isn't the right place after all. Or, in lots of cases, they're over-glamorising an event that would be better experienced informally.

Look for alternatives "When we're sitting in the office, over a formal discussion, they're so busy trying to strike a good bargain, they forget they can ask my advice. When we really get talking and look for alternatives, we usually find a new area of agreement.

"Back at the office, we start talking formally again but we have a new set of criteria to work with. Sometimes this means changing all the figures I've worked on – or even starting at the beginning again with a new idea. But at least I keep the business.

"The strange thing is, I often find these new agreements result in more lasting customers. They come back to me with their business because they know I'll take time to find the right answer for them."

CHECKLIST FOR GETTING IT RIGHT

✓ Look for a new angle to add to the negotiation.
✓ Take a break from negotiations and talk informally.
✓ Find out what the other side really wants to achieve.
✓ Put forward an amended proposal, based on their real needs.
✓ Be prepared to start again with new criteria.

KEEP YOUR 'WANTS' AND 'NEEDS' SEPARATE

'If the fish is on the line, don't let him off.'

It is of the utmost importance, before going into any sort of negotiation, to have established clearly in your mind the various thresholds and cut-off points with regard to your pricing.

1. You need to know your lower limit of 'need'. This is the price below which the sale becomes no longer worth making, even as a loss-leader – this seems obvious enough (though it is amazing how often people fail to have this clearly in their minds). That is the lower limit of 'need'. You should also have, as you will find as we explore the topic further, as thorough a breakdown as possible of how this is calculated. This should include variations in manufacturing costs according to quantities ordered. If you cannot keep all these figures in your head, carry a printout with you in your briefcase.

2. You need to know the upper limit of 'need'. What is less obvious is that it is also worth calculating the point at which the price covers your costs and budgeted profit. That is the upper limit of 'need' and the lower limit of 'want'. And again, as with 1, have a breakdown of how this is calculated.

3. The 'going-in' position. This may well be substantially above 2 (unless the competition is fierce and the product very price-sensitive) but you must never forget the values of 1 or 2 so long as the negotiation continues.

Make your going-in position as high as you dare

How high may 3 be? As high as you dare make it. From 2 upwards you are into the realms of 'want' and you have my best wishes for whatever you can get (so long as I'm not on the other side).

But the principal reason for having 1 and 2 fixed in your mind is that, if negotiations seem to be going incredibly well, and the figures are soaring into the 'want' territory, euphoria can set in. Euphoria has a habit of being attended by amnesia, and an apparently insignificant concession can throw your calculations wildly awry. This is one of the reasons for having the breakdowns with you. And think of the potential for flexibility that you are giving yourself, by being in a position instantly to calculate and offer concessions.

Don't be caught off guard

Another reason is that negotiations can easily wander over many areas, including variations to the specification of the product. If the prospect surprises you with an interest in an increase in quantity well above what was originally under discussion, they will also be looking for a price reduction. What is it to be? Is your memory so good, and are you so adept at mental arithmetic, that you can quickly and safely come back with a revised quote that is preferably no lower than the adjusted 2, and definitely no lower than the adjusted 1?

Of course, you can always cut and run – propose an adjournment for a couple of days while you put together some revised figures – but isn't it a shame to break off when you are on a roll?

The way it works Adjourning can even be disastrous. Food ingredient supplier Humphrey Nelson specialises in small volume, high-margin speciality products, whose high price is offset by quality and lack of waste. That is his 'Unique Selling Point', and he has been very successful. He knows, however, that other, lower-priced products could do the job nearly as well, so he is not without competition.

"On one occasion, a prospect took me completely by surprise with the quantity they were proposing. I thought I'd done my homework thoroughly enough, and prepared a table of prices based on a sliding-scale of gross margin against volume, but the quantities they were talking about went way off my table and I had not brought a breakdown which would have let me extend the table.

"I told them I'd be back by the end of the week with some revised figures. My guardian angel caused me to drive a route the following afternoon right past the prospect's premises. In the visitors' car park I saw the personalised number-plate of an old friend with whom I had been a rookie in the business many years ago, and who now was one of the top salesmen for one of my competitors.

If the fish is on the line, don't let him off "I screeched to a halt down the road, grabbed my mobile telephone, postponed the meeting I was going to, rang the office to get the base-figures I needed, and then feverishly calculated my revisions. I telephoned my secretary, dictated the fresh price-table and a covering letter, and asked her to fax it to the prospect.

"Then I sat and sweated, watching the office car-park. In due course my friend walked out to his car and departed. Immediately I rang my contact in the firm, told him I was in his area, and asked whether he had received the revised figures.

"Ten minutes later, I was in his office, closing the deal. I still don't know how close I came to losing that contract, but I learnt a lesson. Have your numbers ready. And if the fish is on the line, don't let him off."

CHECKLIST FOR GETTING IT RIGHT

✓ Homework: do your sums, and know the thresholds of your profitability.
✓ Have cost breakdowns with you – or, better still, contingency tables.
✓ Don't get carried away by letting apparent success lead you into unaffordable concessions.
✓ If you have to revise your figures, revise them then and there.
✓ Leaving with an intent to return another day is unwise, and could be acutely perilous!

22 | TAKE THE HEAT OFF YOURSELF – RETURN THE ARGUMENT TO THE ISSUE

'If the argument gets personal, make them attack the issue, not you.'

Personal verbal attacks are always unpleasant and can often be quite shocking. They strike at the heart of our self-esteem. As you sit facing another person who, at that moment, strongly dislikes you, it is very difficult to keep functioning properly. Quite often, you will blush as insults or verbal abuse is hurled at you. Blushing makes you feel even worse, because you can't control it and it is a sign of weakness – tangible evidence that the comments have hit home.

Become icy cool and use longer pauses

If you are fortunate not to blush easily, at the first personal insult you must become icy cool in your demeanour and allow longer pauses before you respond. Use the pause to write something – a note of the insult is fine – then make eye contact with your abuser for a few seconds, and respond. This reaction can be quite intimidating and is designed to make the other side worry that they have gone too far. Your response needs to be delivered in a level, calm voice. It should be a statement about the issue.

The way it works

I was discussing a job with a printer who had been a supplier of ours for many years – but only on a small, occasional basis. Most aspects of the job were satisfactory but I was pushing him hard on price. He suddenly exploded! He threw his pencil on the floor, pushed his notepad away and said "I have had enough of you, Missy. You don't care about the people who do this job. You think you are so clever – well you're not..." and it went on in that fairly incoherent way for about two minutes (which felt like a lifetime).

He hit some fairly tender spots in my psyche – I am physically short and I looked quite young at the time. "Missy" reinforced my concern that I did not have enough gravitas to be a negotiator. I was initially too shocked to respond and I turned to look out of the window because I didn't know what else to do. I tried to control my breathing. There was silence in that room for 30 seconds as I sat with a blank face trying to compose myself. This is a very long time.

When I turned back I said "We have to control prices, Peter. Every extra pound per thousand on print prices comes straight off the top. There is nothing I can do to alter that. You, on the other hand can do things which affect the cost of doing the job. Let's look at that".

Switch from the personal remarks to the heart of the issue

I switched attention from the personal attack to the issue. I explained why I was pushing on price (something I hadn't thought to do before) and made no reference at all to his personal comments. Although I didn't know it at the time, this was the best way to handle the situation.

47

If you are a blusher or get visibly flustered, don't worry about it. The situation calls for a different, but no less effective reaction. Again, use silence but instead of looking cool, look disappointed: the sort of look you give to a child who has failed to keep a promise to you. Make notes; you could even mutter "oh dear" under your breath. The silence and your regret again draws attention to the inappropriateness of their behaviour. Keep the silence going for longer than feels bearable. When you do speak, allow your tone to be sad but talk about the issue exactly as I did in the example above.

They may give away their secrets in the heat of the moment

Shifting attention away from personal matters and back to the issue will often be the best you can do, while you struggle to regain your own equilibrium. But, as you become more practised, you can welcome this sort of situation because of the opportunity it can give you to discover more of your opponent's real agenda. In the heat of the moment, much can be given away, and, if you are able to remain cool, you will be able to listen for clues.

In the example above, it was quite clear that the printer (a middle-aged man) was infuriated by having to negotiate with someone younger and female. Almost all his remarks were designed to belittle me. If the outcome of the negotiation had been more important, it might have been wise at that point to bring in an older man from the company to negotiate our corner. The printer would have found it a lot easier to give way on price without losing face.

CHECKLIST FOR GETTING IT RIGHT

✓ Never, ever, fight fire with fire.
✓ The more heated they become, the cooler you should be.
✓ Use a long, long silence after the verbal attack, to draw attention to its stupidity.
✓ When you do speak, make no reference at all to the personal remarks.
✓ Talk about the issue.
✓ If you can, try to pick up clues from the outburst.

23 | BRIDGE THAT GAP WITH EMPATHY

'.. I am sure your Finance Committee will like it...'

People always find it easier to deal with each other if there is some rapport between them. An element of this is evidence of understanding; we like it if people appear to be able to see things from our point of view. Indeed, the greater the differences between two people the more such empathy is appreciated.

The to and fro process of negotiation involves not only a clear vision of what *you* want to achieve, but necessitates the ability to put yourself in someone else's shoes, to some extent; how else are you to make suggestions as trading progresses: "If we agree that it will make things much easier for you in future ..." and know they have some chance of being accepted?

Suggestions may be made either genuinely to balance the deal being struck, or – let us be honest – with ulterior motives. It is what we achieve that matters most. Sometimes, within this process, suggestions can assume – or be made to assume – the form of advice or recommendations. However things are approached, it is essential that a degree of credibility is established.

Building bridges

If everything you suggest is instantly suspect and labelled as a ploy, progress may be difficult or, at worst, deadlock is likely. You cannot conduct negotiations in a manner that sets the participants so far apart that there is no common ground or understanding between you. At the very least, there have to be bridges between what may, in some sense, be adversaries.

Empathy can be a major element in creating such bridges and has particular power to increase credibility.

The way it works

The sequence and logic here is clear:

- Find out about the other person's situation (particularly what their needs are). Note: good questioning techniques are important here – something to check on elsewhere, perhaps.
- Note what you discover.
- Relate your suggestions and comments to what they have told you, using this link to build bridges and increase your credibility.

For example, in a company selling a computer security device (to discourage theft and assist recovery, should it occur), one of their sales team, Peter Ford, is having problems dealing with the I.T. manager of a Chamber of Commerce. The Chamber has a large staff, principally of advisory and administrative people, practically every desk has a PC on it and any loss or damage would not only incur costs (despite insurance) but devastate their operations. Mary Matlock, the I.T. Manager, understands

49

the advantages of the product and wants to order. In what is, frankly, a somewhat bureaucratic organisation, she is struggling to get a deal she knows will be approved by the plethora of committees and decision-making processes involved.

Peter is at pains to discover a bit about the hoops she has to jump through. He asks a number of open questions to encourage her to talk. Not surprisingly she welcomes the enquiry; understanding is important both ways. Gradually, Peter's conversation begins to include more specific reference to the organisational situation that exists:

"... and I am sure your Finance Committee will like it if the figures are shown so that the overall discount is clear ..."

"Now, I remember you saying that your immediate boss is very wary of new products. If you got him to agree to a trial first, the risk is tiny ... and I will still be able to arrange the overall quantity rate despite splitting what you need into two batches ..."

".... if I put all this in writing in a form that can simply be circulated, with just a covering memo from you, that will reduce the work in putting the proposal through the system; on that basis can you ensure it gets considered at the next meeting?"

Thus, he is able to link many of his proposals to statements implying that they are made for her benefit. Because she knows he understands the difficulty of getting approval, she is more likely to accept what he says.

Empathy is a powerful element of the relationship between negotiators. It has broad application throughout the process, but it is at the heartland of the trading that it is most useful. And it is only made possible by setting the scene – and asking questions – early on.

CHECKLIST FOR GETTING IT RIGHT

✓ Ask appropriate questions.
✓ Note what is said in reply.
✓ Watch for opportunities to revisit areas of importance to the other person.
✓ Relate what you say to their situation.
✓ Make the link clear, to establish credibility and build rapport.

SIGNALLING A MOVE BY SAYING NOTHING

'Say what you want . . . without saying a word!'

Many years ago, a famous study by Professor Albert Mehrabian suggested that the following percentages applied to the importance of the three major parts of communication:

- What we say   7%
- How we say what we say   38%
- Body language   55%

Whilst, if this is your first exposure to Mehrabian's thoughts, the 7 per cent for what we say may seem fantastic, years of study support his findings. Regardless of whether you accept Mehrabian or not, however, I'm sure that you would agree that body language has an important part to play in any conversation or negotiation.

They are many times when we wish to indicate a willingness to shift position in our negotiation stance, without verbalising that fact to the other party. This can be done with body language.

Open and closed gestures and postures

The basic rules of body language say that open and closed postures indicate attitudes of mind.

The open posture, body exposed, indicates:

- a willingness to listen;
- a feeling of strength;
- openness of mind;
- possessiveness.

The closed posture, body protected by crossed arms or legs, indicates:

- a defensive attitude;
- a negative attitude;
- an unwillingness to change mind or thought or position.

The basic open and closed gestures are:

Open

Standing or sitting with the body facing the other person. Hands palm up and on show. Head lifted in interest, eyes open. Legs and arms uncrossed.

Closed

Standing or sitting with the body facing away from the other person. Hands palm down or hidden from view. Head down and eyes partly closed or constantly looking away.

Leg crossing

When facing directly to another person, crossed legs can, as discussed, indicate an unwillingness to change one's mind or a defensive, negative position. This meaning, however, can change completely when the seating positions are along side each other. Imagine this situation. You are sitting alongside someone. If they cross their legs towards you they are indicating that they feel comfortable in your company and have a willingness to engage in conversation. If they cross their legs away from you, then the opposite would be the case. You can use this leg-crossing gesture to indicate to another that you are perhaps prepared to change your position in the negotiation. *Provided that you are sitting alongside the other person*, crossing your legs towards them should see a softening of their stance.

Towards and away

Leaning towards another person and entering their space can indicate a willingness to be closer in mind to that person. Conversely, leaning away indicates a 'distancing' from the other person and their views or position. In order to indicate your willingness to change your mental position in a negotiation, change your physical position, by leaning slightly towards the other person. Do not lean too close or this may be perceived as threatening.

The eyes

The level of the upper eyelid is a sure sign of the level of interest a person is showing in response to their environment or the messages they are receiving. The higher the upper eyelid level, the higher the interest. When the upper eyelid is at a level where the white of the eye can be seen above the iris and pupil, the person is indicating shock or surprise. When the eyelid level is between the top of the iris and the top of the pupil, the person is indicating a high level of interest.

When the upper eyelid is at the level of the centre of the pupil the person is indicating a lowering of interest. And when the eyelid has fallen to below the pupil, this indicates boredom or weariness.

Show a willingness to change your position by raising the level of your upper eyelid to the "high interest" level. This small movement will be picked up by the other person, albeit subconsciously, and a change in their positioning should take place.

The lower eyelid

The lower eyelid in its movement upwards and towards the nose, covers the inner canthus of the eye (the small red triangle at the corner of the eye, closest to the nose). When the inner canthus is covered, the person is indicating a concern or disagreement with what has been said. If you wish to indicate to the other person that you have now reached a position in which you would be prepared to discuss a change, ensuring that your inner canthus is always visible is the ideal, non-verbal way of saying so.

CHECKLIST FOR GETTING IT RIGHT

✓ Be aware of your body-language gestures.
✓ Be aware of the other party's body-language gestures.
✓ Use open body postures to indicate a willingness to hear more.
✓ Use 'towards' positioning to indicate a willingness to move.
✓ Use open eyes.
✓ Ensure the inner canthi of your eyes remain visible.

25 HOW TO INTERPRET THE 'GREEN LIGHT' SIGNAL

'When a decision is made, the negotiator will relax back in the chair.'

When all of the hard work is done and you have found the basis of an agreement, all can still be lost if you miss the signal to agree and keep on negotiating. Only do and say enough to get the 'green light' and nothing else, until the deal is done.

Put your opposite number at ease

Building rapport with your opponent quickly and naturally is the most important skill a negotiator has to possess: the better you are at being in rapport with another person the greater will be your ability to spot comfort and discomfort with points in your negotiations. The more you put your opposite number at ease, the more relaxed they will become and show more of the body's in-built communication system. If you can read these signs, you will know when a product or service seems too much to pay or a specific point of the negotiation is more appealing than another.

As you advance through your negotiations, gathering as much information as possible and only agreeing to points if they are matched with an agreement in return, watch very carefully for eye and body movements: if you make a statement or answer a question that causes the other party to spring forward in his or her seat, you will probably realise that you have touched on a point that is of interest. If all signs were this obvious, negotiators would have a very easy life.

Look for the non-verbal signs

Most signs of non-verbal communication are much more subtle than that but can be watched for and, with practice, identified, with increasing accuracy. Usually, any folded-arm or crossed-leg gestures are generally not 'green light' signals, but an open arm with palm up, on the other hand, usually signals a degree of ease, both with you and with your propositions. Any 'towards' motions are a sign that you have raised a point of interest and you should then ask an open question, to explore more about what interested them in the point that you have just made. If you can identify a point of extreme interest, most of the other issues have less relevance and a go-ahead can be asked for whilst briefly covering such trivial matters as price.

During the course of the negotiations, there will come a point when your counterpart will reach a decision. If they have already decided to go ahead with the deal but you are negotiating the finer points, you will have done enough to satisfy his needs.

Are they relaxed?

In most cases, one of the strongest 'green light' signs, or signals that a decision has been reached, is that the person you are dealing with will become relaxed; whilst they are contemplating their mind is working and their body will reflect this: they will be alert and sitting upright. When they have made a decision, they relax back in their chair and, as their mind slows down their body will relax. However, this may not necessarily mean that you have an agreement: if they relax back, cross their arms and feign interest in other things on the desk, this would suggest that you have more work to do. At this stage, do not ask for an outright agreement to go ahead but ask general questions about which parts of the agreement they like and which part they are not so keen on.

Alter their posture to alter their way of thinking

This re-questioning should also be accompanied by an action that forces the other person to alter their posture, such as handing them a piece of paper or leaning forward to ask them to look at a letter or piece of information; this will make them uncross their arms, to take hold of the item you are drawing their attention to. If you can alter their posture in this way, it will become easier to alter their way of thinking .

When you see the change in posture, if it is accompanied by eye contact and perhaps a smile or even nodding of the head, you can be more sure that the decision should be a favourable one. At this stage, you should ask for an agreement to continue to the next negotiation point or for an agreement to go ahead with the whole deal. Once you have asked for an agreement, say nothing. Until you have obtained a response, you must resist the urge to interrupt any silences and start reiterating key points. You must only give enough information, or concede enough points at the negotiation stage, to secure an agreement. If you go on conceding even minor points or adding extra value after someone has decided to go ahead, you will only go on to devalue your product or service.

CHECKLIST FOR GETTING IT RIGHT

✓ Only do and say enough to get the green light and nothing else, until the deal is done.
✓ Building rapport will help you to spot comfort and discomfort points in your negotiations.
✓ Watch eye and body movements carefully.
✓ When they are relaxed, it usually means they have reached a decision.
✓ Make your questions indirect: "which part of the agreement do you like?".
✓ A change in posture helps to change their way of thinking.
✓ Once you have asked for an agreement, say nothing.

26 | SMILE PLEASE – THE POWER AND INFLUENCE OF SMILING

'... it doesn't mean I am trying to stitch you up.'

There is a classic poster from the 'Peanuts' cartoons, of a bemused Snoopy contemplating his devastated kennel; it has the simple caption "Never trust a smiling cat". Yet here we consider the power of a smile to invoke positive responses – including trust. Smiling is not to be dismissed as a clichéd approach. It works; and can influence things generally, throughout the course of a negotiation, or at a specific moment.

As such, a smile is a technique that can be used in many different ways, for example to:

- create a pause and get a word in;
- provoke questions (voiced or not);
- provoke comment (or additional information);
- create a smokescreen;
- give you time to think;
- influence the moment or the longer term;
- change or amend how you come over.

Instant or later effect

As has been said, the time here can be long or short. For instance, just a smile and an exclamation: "Oh, come on!" may act to get someone to revisit a point and give you more information. In another way it might be intended to influence the course of events in the longer term. Clearly it must always be carefully used. Saying something like: "Trust me, this will be just what you want," accompanied by a glib smile, may be self-destructive: you are instantly typecast as *not* to be trusted. But it can work. In the example that follows, a simple interjection into the conversation is shown helping secure an agreement on a particular point, and influencing not only the rest of the negotiation, but also relationships beyond it.

The way it works

Mary Taylor and Jane Fenton are colleagues. Well, they will be. Garwana Financial has merged with the smaller company for which Jane used to work. Their respective departments are combining and the two of them are sitting down to negotiate who will do what – there are many details to be arranged and agreed, from where everyone will be located to who will accept voluntary redundancy. The two have met only two or three times and there are still many things to be finalised; but one thing is certain, the two must find a way to work together effectively in future.

During another meeting, Mary lays out a suggestion regarding staff locations (in fact dictated as much as anything by the way a variety of I.T. equipment and systems have to be installed). Jane is still very defensive (after all it was once her department; all be it a small one). "I really think this will cause my team real inconvenience" she starts, "and it is just one more change which will … ".

She falters into silence as she sees Mary smile broadly. Mary uses the pause to interrupt: "Just because I am called Taylor", she says, "it doesn't mean I want to stitch you up!" She continues without pause, but still in a friendly manner: "We both know this isn't ideal – putting in all this new equipment means there are real constraints – but think how useful it is going to be, for example ..." (and she offers just one advantage, which means locations will be less important anyway).

It changed the tone   It was hardly the quip of the year, but an unexpected smile and a light comment certainly acted to change the tone of the meeting and, maybe, its likely development. One might be cynical and suggest that Mary was *only* smiling as a ploy. But the two women have to work together, so, assuming Mary knew what she was about, it is perhaps much more likely that she had two purposes here:

- To break the chain of suspicion and disgruntled reactions, which was threatening to prevent the meeting from covering matters constructively.

- To begin (or continue or be part of) a process designed to create what will become an ongoing creative and constructive (and pleasant) working relationship between the two. It is a start if Jane begins to see Mary, not as a sort of executioner, but as human; someone she can work with – even if her sense of humour is not yet being shown to be exceptional!

CHECKLIST FOR GETTING IT RIGHT

✓ Do not let sour relationships inhibit negotiation.
✓ Look for an opportunity to use a smile (or joke) to change the atmosphere.
✓ Ensure you project a human face.
✓ Link the hiatus to a restart of the conversation – with you leading.
✓ Make sure what comes next makes sense to the other person (and justifies the restart).

5 NICE SURPRISES

PACK YOUR BAGS AND GO ...

'... a powerful tactic, if you choose the right moment ...'

There are very few times in a negotiating situation where things become so desperate, you want to pack up and go. But if you're faced with an ultimatum – a 'take-it-or-leave-it' situation – then you may have no choice.

In fact, this can be a very powerful tactic – if you choose the right moment and if you don't use it too often. If they really want your business or your co-operation, they'll come after you with a better offer.

The main rule is – don't use this tactic until you've tried everything else you know. But if you do get to a point where the other side won't budge from their position and won't negotiate with you, call a halt.

Avoid confrontation

This doesn't have to be confrontational. If they're on your home ground, tell them the discussion is at an end but that they can contact you any time if they decide they would like to negotiate.

If you're on their territory, stay calm and in control, and say you feel there's nothing to be gained from carrying on the discussion. Just pick up your papers and leave. But don't forget to hand them your card in case they should change their minds and want to talk again in the future.

Don't use this if there's still a chance of negotiation

Never use this tactic in anger, unless you're prepared to lose what you're bargaining for completely. And don't do it if you think there's still a chance you might reach an amicable agreement. But if you really reach a deadlock, where you have nothing to lose and you're prepared to gamble on the other side wanting your business enough to give in, you have little alternative.

The way it works

Simon is managing director of an up-and-coming woodcraft company that is successfully expanding its retail outlets. He says he would never have got anywhere if he accepted all the 'take-it-or-leave-it' deals that were offered to him.

"I don't give up easily – but I do know when I'm beaten" he says, "and being beaten doesn't mean you have to accept conditions where you come out the loser. Whatever your deal is about, there's always another supplier or another alternative if you look for it.

Calculate the alternatives

"So, when things really look like they're going wrong, I make a quick calculation, by asking myself two questions I think are vital. Am I losing out on other business by wasting my time here, when I know there can be nothing more to gain? And can I afford to reject the offer that's on the table at the moment? If the answer to both questions is 'yes' then I pack up and go.

"But I don't take that step before I'm very sure there can be no further negotiation – either on price or on other concessions that would make the deal worthwhile. And then I don't close the door on a future deal. I always leave my business card. And if I don't hear from them I give them a call a week or so later, to see if they've changed their minds.

Don't bluff unless you're prepared to lose

"Of course, I know there are some importers who sell reasonably but can still bring their prices down and it's tempting to walk out on them as a bluff – to see if they can be scared into coming after me with a better price. I only try this if I'm really confident I'll be able to go back to them at a later date if it doesn't work – or that I can get the wood elsewhere.

"You only get so many chances to use this one. If you get a reputation for walking out on negotiations, the tactic loses its impact."

 ## CHECKLIST FOR GETTING IT RIGHT

✓ Only walk out on a negotiation as a last resort.
✓ If they issue an ultimatum – 'take it or leave it' – you have little alternative.
✓ Make sure you can't negotiate on things other than price.
✓ Calculate your alternatives – can you afford to walk out?
✓ Make it easy for them to come back to you – avoid confrontation.
✓ Don't use this as a bluff unless you're prepared to lose.

28 | THE 'YES AT ANY PRICE' SURPRISE

'Watch out for those extras ...'

Nine times out of ten, price is the key issue in any negotiation. When you are preparing to negotiate you will be discussing with your colleagues how high (or low) you are prepared to go. When you are in the negotiating meeting, you know that the other side will be thinking about price all the time. It may not be discussed immediately as you both jockey for the position of power but you know that price is what it will all boil down to in the end.

In fact, a negotiation can often carry on for hours with everyone skirting around making an offer, because you each want the other to reveal their hand first.

Knock the other side off balance

This tactic is designed to speed things up, put you in total control and knock the other side slightly off balance, because it is so unexpected.

Your response to their first, ridiculously low offer is "Yes, OK!" You then continue "Quite frankly, you can pay us whatever you want, within reason, for this. Let's see how it works".

The rest of the negotiation is handled by you using their initial offer as a base price. Every activity connected with delivering the product or service is treated as an 'extra' and has a price attached.

The way it works

Daley & Co. wanted 2000 quality fountain pens to give to their customers as an incentive to increase order value. They had called in Incentives Unlimited to discuss supply. The catalogue price was £6.50 per pen although Incentives Unlimited had, somewhat unwisely, said "Ignore the catalogue price" early in the meeting. Daley and Co. wanted a quick meeting and a keen price so their buyer said "Right, these pens are going out as incentives so we can't afford to spend much. For 2000 pens I can offer you £1000." Incentives Unlimited could have started counter bargaining on price, by talking about how expensive they were to produce, the quality, the available margins and then suggested £4 per pen.

Instead, the rep. said "Yes, OK. You can pay 50 pence for each pen. Let's see how it works."

Daley & Co. were delighted. "Good. Now, we want them delivered in three weeks to this address". "Will you be wanting nibs with them?" enquired the Incentives Unlimited rep. "Of course!" replied Daley & Co. "And each in its own protective tube?" "Er ... yes", came the slightly cautious reply. "Now what sort of finish do you want? Standard, enamel or tortoiseshell?" "Oh, they must be dark blue", the buyer insisted. The discussion continued in this vein for some time, with the Incentives Unlimited rep. taking copious notes.

Adding in the extras

Finally, he put down his pen and said "Right, I think I have got everything. Here is the breakdown. Pen at 50 pence, gold nib at £1.80 (stainless steel comes in at 10 pence less if you want but I don't recommend it: it just doesn't say quality the way gold does), dark-blue enamel barrel at 65 pence, standard protective plastic tube at 28 pence (the perspex presentation boxes with your logo printed on would look terrific but they cost a bit more at £1.50), delivery and insurance (which is mandatory) is 46 pence, ink cartridges at 32 pence ... that comes in at £4.01 all in. I'm delighted that I can keep it this low, it's because of the volume, of course".

The Daley & Co. buyer had to smile. His low-price bluff had been well and truly called and the Incentives Unlimited rep. had made a counter offer that was very hard to fight. This tactic is quite useful when you are forced into making an offer first.

Spot the give-away

Miriam was trying to sell her company and she found herself in the position of having to say how much she wanted for it. She still had no real understanding of what it would be worth to the other side and was worried that she was going to ask for too little. So she reached for a figure which was three times turnover, because that was what her accountant had suggested.

When the other side said "Yes, well, I think there is something to discuss there" she knew that she had pitched too low. This man had a reputation for throwing his arms in the air and declaring that a price was "impossible" so this mild reaction was a give-away.

"Good" she replied, "Now, as you can see, stock has been independently valued at £100,000 and the customer database is on two Everex cubes, which are owned by a sister company and valued at £16,000". The list of "extras" ranging from buying out the buildings lease to training the new owners in the computerised sales and warehousing programmes added another 50 per cent onto her original price.

 ## CHECKLIST FOR GETTING IT RIGHT

✓ Always prepare thoroughly, if you are going to use this tactic.
✓ Work out a breakdown of extras and their prices, so that you can adjust them to fit the end price you want to achieve.
✓ Play it with a completely straight face.
✓ Feed in alternatives in the areas where you would be happy to give way a little.

HANDLING THE SIDE-STEPPED QUESTION

"Answer it for them and wait."

In nearly every negotiation, there are key pieces of information which you need to find out from the other party, in order clearly to understand their position, views, feelings and reasons for negotiating with you. You may also need this information so that you can apply or resist pressure and identify issues which need to be 'on the table' before you can get down to the open and forthright discussion. What do you do if they decide they don't want to answer your question or try to side-step it?

Preparation Preparation is important. Before you negotiate, list the key issues as they affect you and draw up a list of things you need to establish with the other party, before you get into the detailed process of bargaining and compromise. Having drawn up this list, start with broad, non-directed, open questions. This will give little away about where your real interest might be and may get the other party talking more openly. This will provide you with early clues as to the 'real' situation.

Persevere Move from non-directed, open questions to more specific questions on the broad issues. Persevere. It is at this point that you will start to notice whether they try to side-step you. When it happens, ask the question again but be even more direct. Do this without becoming aggressive in your approach. Keep it calm and relaxed. If your questions are still side-stepped, do three things:

- Note the questions being side-stepped. This, in itself, is a clear indication that you have touched on areas of the discussion that are sensitive.
- Back off and approach the same issue a little later from another direction.
- Use information that you already have to imply that you already know the answer; therefore, they aren't going to make their position any weaker by answering your question.

If necessary be direct For example, you are negotiating with a company to win an order from them. The market is very competitive and, before agreeing to any terms of business, you need to find out whether they are dealing with your competitors. You decide to ask "Are you talking to other companies about your requirements?". You know they must be but you want to find out which of your competitors. They side-step the question. A little later, be more direct by referring to one of your competitors in a general way. See if the other party responds. Your next question might be along the lines "I've noticed that Company X is very active in the marketplace at the moment with their range of ... but one or two others in the market are less active. What do you think?".

The more the other party tries to evade your questions the more direct you need to be. "Are you talking to Company X?".

Observe their reactions

While you are doing this watch their reactions. In particular, watch their eyes. There will be several possible reactions.

- They may look down or seem slightly uncomfortable.
- They may smile slightly.
- They may react by more strongly side-stepping your question.

At this point they have answered your question by the way they have reacted. Yes, they are talking to Company X.

Use silence

Another tactic is to use silence. This can be very useful in applying pressure. Ask a question and then keep quiet until it is answered. It is very difficult for the other party to remain silent if they have been asked a question and then there is a silent expectation that they should answer. Often, they become increasingly uncomfortable and they are forced to say something. Again start with more wide-ranging, open questions and become more and more direct. To have the maximum effect, you will need to be more direct more quickly.

For example: "This is a major purchase you are considering. You must be speaking to other companies about this. Which ones in particular?". You keep quiet and wait for them to reply.

The way it works

Ted Wainwright went to Japan for the first time just over ten years ago. He needed to identify a major Japanese company that was interested in purchasing products which his company was well known for outside Japan. It was important for Ted that he find a Japanese company that would be willing to enter into a long-term arrangement with him. Numerous meetings took place with five companies but one seemed more interesting than the rest. However, it seemed strange to Ted that, although they were keen to enter the marketplace, they hadn't already done so. This suggested that they might still be talking to other companies. By a process of elimination, Ted knew they must be talking to either a Belgian competitor or several in the USA. At each meeting, Ted kept trying to find which ones. They side-stepped. "I was getting frustrated so I decided to be direct (a difficult thing to try in Japan!). I assumed they were talking to the Belgian company and said that this company was very good. They agreed! I then asked them why, if the Belgian company was very good, they were talking to my company? They mentioned a weakness in the product specification and I was in."

CHECKLIST FOR GETTING IT RIGHT

✓ Be prepared for the side-step.
✓ Persevere, becoming more direct in your approach.
✓ Watch their reactions.

30 | WHY BEGINNING AT THE BEGINNING IS NOT ALWAYS BEST

'You can condition the other party into saying yes ...'

Being creative in your approach to opening negotiations can very often make the whole negotiation situation easier to control and allow you to draw certain assumptions before getting to the finer points.

Be different and stand out from the crowd

Although starting at the beginning may seem the most logical, it may not be the best place to start. In situations where you are competing against other suppliers, appearing different may prove advantageous and allow you to stand out from the crowd.

If you start with a minor point, which would normally be dealt with towards the end of the negotiations, for example, the siting of a piece of the equipment, to give their answer, they will have to visualise the product in its place and, therefore, mentally assume that they already own the equipment.

Starting at a minor point also allows you time to become accustomed to the person you are entering into negotiations with, and therefore build rapport. If it is someone that you already know, you can discover their mood and, in each case, find out a little of how much your product or service is needed.

Get them relaxed – they will give away more

There is a further advantage. As you have not yet dived into the negotiations and started trying to agree price, or delivery, or specifications, your counterpart may still be in a semi-relaxed state – and likely to give away more information than if they had already donned their negotiator's cap. Once you start asking for major decisions to be made, then the 'down to business' programme runs through the brain and, from then on, information has to be prised from them and friendliness is reduced.

Beginning with a minor point allows you to condition the other party into saying 'yes'. By carefully plotting your course, you can get your first 'yes' from something that is painfully obvious: "do you need this new photocopier to replace the one that is broken?". Then the next question can be asked which may need slightly more thought but will hopefully prompt a 'yes' answer: "will the new machine be sited in the same position?". "So you are looking for a machine of about the same dimensions?"

Condition them to say 'yes'

The more often you are able to get them to say 'yes' and agree small points that would usually be thrown away after the negotiations were completed, the more accustomed they will become to agreeing with you. By doing this, you raise your chances of smoothly getting the final 'yes' when you need a decision to go ahead.

64

Small jumps make it easier to agree the whole deal

Linking together a series of questions (each of them increasing slightly in importance) also makes it easier for them to make the final step of agreeing the whole deal. It is much easier for people to make what they consider small jumps, when making decisions, rather than one large one. To achieve this, you will need to incorporate the questions as part of your conversation. Avoid an 'intensive' questioning style, which is likely to put your opponent on the defensive.

This form of negotiation is a lot more laborious than going straight for the kill but some people need to make it appear that the decision is an important one. This enhances their own importance as such an important decision must only be made by an 'important person'. In these cases it is better to play to their fantasies rather than trying to take the short cuts.

If the subject of your negotiations is a product or service that you market on a regular basis, a good idea is to spend time planning the order of points to be negotiated. Then, if you change the order in which you cover each point, this will enable you to discover the most effective way of starting and completing your negotiations.

CHECKLIST FOR GETTING IT RIGHT

✓ If you're in a competitive position, being different is advantageous.
✓ Get them to imagine the product already in place.
✓ Use their semi-relaxed state at the beginning to make them give away information.
✓ Get them used to saying 'yes' to the easy questions.
✓ Get them to 'yes' by making the jumps easy to make.

"OH, BY THE WAY..."

'Use an afterthought as a lever'

Like, salami, the negotiated deal may be served in thin slices. Laying all our cards on the table right at the start is rarely the best option; new demands can be made progressively throughout the process. Ultimately, of course, both parties have to agree the deal, but here is a technique which can often act to secure a final element (or two), swinging the final balance in your favour just a little more.

Cumulative agreement

At the end of the day, all the parties to a negotiation must make up their minds: is it a deal – a package – they can accept? But judgment is not left until the last minute, the developing deal is constantly assessed, as various components are agreed. Thus, at any particular moment, someone has a view on 'how it looks, so far'.

This is natural human behaviour; indeed, it would be difficult to suspend all judgment until the end. But it gives this technique a good chance of success. Once the deal is 'stacking up well' an increasing reluctance to let it founder develops. This is especially so when the deal is complex or takes a long time to thrash out; or both.

Just one more thing

So, what is done here is that something you want is saved and only brought out at a late stage – at which point, agreement is more likely if it appears that everything achieved so far might be wasted without it. More than one thing can be introduced in this way (beware of overdoing it: more than a certain number of 'final' points may strain your credibility and cause a backlash!). And such points may be different in type. For example, they may be genuinely minor, or not; or even contentious and important. What will work at this stage depends on your skills, the nature of the other party and the point in question. Judge carefully; and learn from experience.

The way it works

Charles Foot is in charge of international operations for a company making machine tools. He has teams of engineers working on projects in a dozen countries, an activity that gives rise to a requirement for hundreds of hotel nights every year – and costs a great deal of money. He is negotiating a corporate deal with a sales executive – Jayne – from an international hotel group.

They are near to agreement, and a long list of variables has been discussed: room rates; their link to the number of room-nights taken; global versus country rates; the inclusion – or not – of breakfast; the ability to use fax and computer equipment in the rooms. Charles is driving a hard bargain and Jayne, who wants the business and is prepared to discount and make an arrangement to get it, has been led to believe that

A deal that saves money and will be popular

he is concerned primarily with cost, which is indeed important. At last she summarises, confident that the deal is now set, but Charles has not finished: "There's just one thing", he says "this all looks quite good, but it would only be acceptable if it applied to Executive grade rooms; I could certainly agree it on that basis". Jayne is nonplussed. They had discussed the various levels of room available and he had appeared to be uninterested in anything but the best price on the standard room "let's just review what you can do in standard, I am after making some savings here". She sees the possibility of the whole discussion opening up again, and, after a certain amount of protest, agrees "on that basis". Charles is pleased: "Right, that looks good, it is a lot of business we are talking about here, after all. Our own plans mean it should be more in future too – Oh, by the way, I meant to mention checkout time. I imagine there would be no problem extending that till, say, six in Asia, where our people return home on flights in the evening". It looks like being a deal that will not just save money, but be one his people will like.

CHECKLIST FOR GETTING IT RIGHT

✓ Select things that lend themselves to late mentioning.
✓ Minimise their importance, yet make the deal seem dependent on the new overall agreement implied.
✓ Watch for linked subsidiary points; you might get away with more than one.
✓ Assess the meeting as it progresses, in case you change your mind; there might be a case for avoiding this technique.
✓ Don't overdo it.

6 DEVIOUS AND DIRTY TACTICS

'The conditional 'yes' is the cornerstone of effective negotiation.'

The word 'yes' is a powerful one in the negotiation situation. For years, sales people have known that if you can get a prospect to say 'yes' to a number of unimportant issues during the preliminary part of a sales situation, they are much more likely to agree to the final proposition. In negotiation, too, this works in a surprisingly effective way. You have, therefore, to be careful when the opposition starts working this tactic with you. Be wary of the opponent who is too nice, who is too friendly and gets you agreeing to seemingly unimportant items in too comfortable a fashion. It may be that the 'sting' is just around the corner! The conditional 'yes' is the cornerstone of effective negotiation. Get into the habit of asking yourself "if I say 'yes' to this issue for the opposition, what do I want them to do for me?".

Only use 'yes' as a conditional response

Establish the habit of always qualifying any 'yes' you give with a secondary statement. Even if you are agreeing to having another cup of coffee, make sure when you reply that you say something along the lines "yes, but not too strong" just to soften the 'yes' response. If you do this then you will be preparing the way for any other qualified 'yes but subject to' statements.

Become a 'nibbler'

One of the ways you can increase the value of any deal to yourself is to become a 'nibbler'. Whenever you say 'yes' add something like "provided that includes..." or "and I assume that includes ...". In this way, you can often add up to 10 per cent to the value of any deal without the other side realising what you are doing!

Think package!

John had been wanting to change his office PC for sometime. Compared with those he used in his clients' offices, his machine was now incredibly slow and it would not run the new software that was becoming the industry standard. When he approached the computer-supply company he normally used, he was taken aback by the cost of the newer, faster machines. When he worked out all the numbers, the cost was well over budget, even with the normal company discount.

In good negotiator style, he had made the decision to walk away from the deal when the 'phone rang and it was the computer supplier with a proposition he found difficult to refuse. One of their customers had just cancelled an order for three machines of the exact specification that John had decided upon. However, the price was still outside what John had to spend in terms of the whole system. The basic machine, however, was 10 per cent less than his budget, so after a lengthy discussion John said 'yes' to the deal, provided that a service agreement was included together with a substantial package of software, a colour printer and a number of support items, the cost of which would have added up to substantially more than the budget.

A truly win-win solution

Let's think what happened here. The supplier was embarrassed by the cancelled order and could afford to include several items which, although they did not cost the supplier much money, were worth a considerable amount to John. John could have simply been delighted at the 10 per cent discount and paid full price for the other items. However, by using the 'qualified yes' he gained exactly the system he was looking for at a price he could afford. A truly 'win-win' solution for both sides.

CHECKLIST FOR GETTING IT RIGHT

✓ Beware the opponent who gets you saying 'yes' to simple things too quickly. They may be going for a quick kill!
✓ Whenever you are going to say 'yes', make sure it is a qualified 'yes'. What else can you ask for at the same time?
✓ Rather than the basic item or service you are buying, think in terms of the complete package. What additional items can you ask for that will not cost the supplier as much as they will cost you?
✓ Use the 'yes' technique to push your own side of the deal. Get the other side used to saying 'yes' to inconsequential items and only use the 'conditional yes' yourself.
✓ Assess the power base of the other side. What pressures do you think are on the opposition for them to complete the deal?
✓ Become a 'nibbler' and see what value you can add to the deal by qualifying your 'yes' responses.

WHEN IT DOESN'T PAY TO BACK DOWN ON PRICE!

'Concede once and you will be forced to concede again.'

Negotiate price out of the equation

In a market place where more and more businesses are competing purely on a cost basis, fewer businesses are succeeding at differentiating themselves from their competition. It is rare to see a business succeeding on value added-service or a Unique Selling Proposition (USP), allowing them to command a higher price. This has led to more and more negotiations and tenders being driven primarily by cost.

Whilst most businesses accept the notion that 'you get what you pay for', the economic climate is such that cash is king and long-term investments are increasingly difficult to justify. In this context, selling and negotiating terms for a high-value, high-priced product or service is exceptionally difficult. The key to success is all about framing the outcome and positioning the product or service correctly, right up front. If you believe in what you do and what you sell, do not get involved in cutting the price in order to compete.

Cost-cutting is an approach that will lead to a squabble between the tendering suppliers and will not allow you to elevate yourself above the pack. The technique described below will assist you in avoiding the catch-22 that is price-cutting and remember, once you start to cut your price you are making a millstone to hang round your own neck.

Framing the outcome and avoiding price concessions

Framing the outcome during a negotiation will allow you to take the issue of cost out of the equation. Cost only becomes significant when the investment is more than the perceived value or benefit that your product or service will bring to your customer's business.

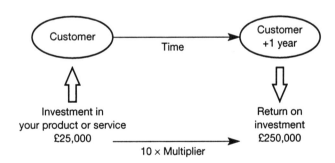

Figure 33.1 Framing the outcome

71

Four points to agree

The above model shows this in action. To frame the outcome, you need to agree with your customer, as part of the negotiation:

- the quantifiable bottom-line savings;
- the increases in production;
- the increases in sales or ...
- whatever business performance gains they will realise, as a result of investing in your products or services.

To achieve this, ask them what they believe they will gain as a business from your product or service and ask them to put a monetary value on it. For example, you are selling manufacturing consultancy that will save two pence per unit.

Discuss what you will deliver as part of your consultancy package and get them to agree that a two-pence saving per unit is a reasonable amount. Ask them how many units they produce per year.

In this example, they are producing 12,500,000 units per year, which corresponds to a £250,000 saving. As a full package, the investment to secure twenty-five days of your company's consultancy corresponds to a £25,000 investment. This relates to a ten times multiplier on their investment. Now for the best bit. Not only are you sure that they will realise this saving but you are so confident that you are willing to offer them a money-back guarantee. If they do not realise the savings you are talking about, then you will refund their money in full. Suddenly you have framed and positioned the outcome in such a way that price is not a factor.

In this negotiating environment, you do not have to worry about conceding price at all. In fact, you can turn a request for a price-cut to your advantage. How do you achieve this?

Exclusivity: your unique selling proposition (USP)

Imagine that this is the USP for the manufacturing consultancy business used in the example above:

"Most consultants offer you a high-cost solution to a manufacturing problem and do not guarantee the outcome of their work. We invest just the right amount of time in your business so that we can guarantee the solution we will provide. And not only will we guarantee it, if we do not meet the benchmarks we have agreed together, then we will offer you a money-back guarantee. This means that doing business with us is a no-risk option – we *will* deliver you the results your business deserves."

This is a pretty exclusive arrangement and you can tell your prospect or customer that they have been specifically selected as a business that may benefit from your services. By negotiating in this framework you can effectively *demand* to be taken seriously – as long as your business can deliver the results you are offering. If they ask for a price-cut under this framework, they are not taking you seriously, so be prepared to abandon the negotiation.

This technique is massively powerful during a tendering process, especially if there are multiple aspects to the contract and you want it all. The best way to illustrate this is through an example from our business.

Applying the technique

William Carpenter, one of our sales people, recently made a call on a large business which wanted development training in four areas:

- leadership;
- change-management;
- strategic communications; and
- self-directed work teams.

After some discussion with the prospect, William positioned the concept that the development programme should be based around a hub of core skills that ran through all four areas. At this point, the prospect pointed out that there were four companies bidding and they might mix and match the suppliers. They advised that it would not be sensible for us to integrate the programme into one deliverable.

Jumping at the chance to describe our approach to people- and business-development, William advised the prospect that this was not the way we did things.

William described how we guaranteed the outcome for the customer and, whilst we are expensive, we deliver a whole solution to a business problem, not a menu to be selected from. Only by managing the whole process, can we guarantee the results. William went on to suggest that perhaps we were not the right company to be asking to bid and was prepared to leave. The prospect was bowled over by this approach and it really did position our business well.

CHECKLIST FOR GETTING IT RIGHT

✓ Frame the outcome – take price out of the equation.
✓ Use your USP to elevate your business out of the price war.
✓ Use risk-reversal, by offering a money-back guarantee on your products and services.
✓ Be prepared to leave if price is still the major issue ... let them deal with *SuperSave*!

34 MANAGING THE ONES WHO TRY TO GRIND YOU DOWN

'... meeting after meeting, the negotiations go on and on without a conclusion.'

The problem!

The process of doing business with someone who continuously tries to grind you down to the last penny or bleed you dry of everything they can get from you, will eventually drive you away. What can you do to prevent this from happening and spoiling what could well become an excellent relationship for all concerned? It's even more infuriating when negotiations drag on seemingly forever.

Tactical options

1. Begin by accepting that you're never going to deal with everyone, or even want to!
2. Have a firm point beyond which, if pushed, you are prepared to walk away.
3. Find out from the other side just how much they do want to work with you!
4. Shame them into changing their tactics, as all they are serving to do is make it impossible for you to work together. Ask them to explain why you have so many meetings that never seem to get anywhere and propose an alternative schedule to get things going again.
5. You may choose to appeal to their fair-sided nature by opening up and disclosing the numbers involved. Often they won't push beyond this, because they can see that they're making it impossible for you to be able to meet their unrealistic expectations. When this happens they will either stop there or request for negotiations to continue in the light of this new information.
6. You can toughen up and hit the other side with demands, putting them on the defensive. Now you'll know if you were ever in with a chance of getting the deal.
7. Get some inside information on their true intentions in dealing with you and who is your competition. In most circumstances, you'll have an ally within the other side's business: ask for help. Devise a strategy on how to deal with them and get what you want, without giving too much away.
8. Show the other side that you are in no rush and could live without this deal. When they see you're not buckling under their pressure or delaying tactics, see how long it is before they become easier to work with to conclude negotiations.
9. At the start ensure everyone is working to a clearly defined and agreed agenda. At the close of each meeting, make sure everyone knows what action is required of them by the next meeting. This will help drive the process faster, as excuses become more difficult to create.
10. Schedule a timetable of decisions: should you find they are abusing it, this is a clear indicator of what's likely to come in the future, so be careful.

Please remember, there is nothing you want so much that you want it at any price, or that you cannot find it elsewhere, or have to put up with other people being allowed to waste your time and money. Each day spent with someone wasting your time keeps you away from someone who will want to work with you.

The way it works

When sales director Andrew Davey was pushed up to an alleged time limit by his client for over £70,000 worth of new office furniture he recognised that he was being ground down by requests for price-reduction and free upgrades on certain items. The time had come for Andrew to re-establish a level playing field.

Andrew called for one final meeting to present his final position. At the appointed time the meeting began and Andrew apologised, saying that, due to an error in his estimating department, the cost was in fact going to have to go up! This caused deep breathing amongst the other side, who were clearly expecting a price reduction. Now faced with the price going up the other side began negotiating with Andrew to keep to the original price in the proposal. Reluctantly, Andrew agreed on the basis that agreement to proceed was reached today. He got the deal.

It's not always going to go in your favour but, if you really want to halt the grinding-down process, it pays to make a stand from time to time; walk away, if necessary, and find the people you want to work with, not those out after all they can get.

CHECKLIST FOR GETTING IT RIGHT

✓ Always work to an agreed agenda.
✓ At each stage, ensure you are aware of exactly what is expected.
✓ Don't be afraid to shame them when they're being unrealistic in their demands.
✓ Appeal, if necessary, to their better nature and fairmindedness.
✓ You can even put some demands of your own on the table.
✓ There is nothing you want at any price.
✓ Be prepared to remove your offer.
✓ Walk away, rather than let the other side drain your cash.

35

USING COMPETITORS' PROPS TO INFLUENCE THE OUTCOME

'Why do so many businesses invest in the use of props? Because they work.'

In today's ever-increasing and competitive marketplace, you need to make use of any and all opportunities that come to hand. One such method is that of utilising inanimate objects to help persuade and guide clients' or suppliers' decisions to deal with you and your business. Take care, however, not to overplay your hand, the alternative being a decision against you.

What can be used?

The list can become lengthy, as there is a use for almost anything if you think about it long enough. Perhaps some of the key objects below will provide an insight. With each object comes a way you may be able to use it.

Competitor quotation

Leaving it on your desk may seem a little obvious, but placing it to one side can look as though it's been there for some time. The idea is that when your supplier enters, they see the file there as something you are working on and this generally does put them on their toes. You want them to be aware that you are serious about buying and that you are talking to others in order to get the best deal. They are then pressured to come in with a more competitive offer for your business.

Reception

Another intimidating gesture is to place competitor's information, literature and even annual reports at your reception. Upon entry, what's the first thing they see?

Signing in!

A bit cheeky, but I have known companies to sign in at their reception a competitor who has been there the day before. Between this and the literature, your point is made. By now, the signals are strong enough to ensure you have a competitive lead for the negotiations ahead.

Walkabout

Try a pre-negotiating meeting walkabout. Set up competitor's products that can be seen, and make it look as though this is an impromptu opportunity for them to see what you do before you begin. Talk about what everyone else is doing to help you and drop hints as to what you will be looking for from today.

Collect your own!

It's good advice to look at what items you can collect from customers and suppliers alike. You'll never know just when you will need them to help you in a negotiating situation. Ask for items such as:

- annual reports;
- literature/newsletters;
- product samples;
- desk pads/pens;
- clocks;
- wall charts/posters;
- certificates/awards;

- a video to display in your reception;
- screen savers.

The way it works

An example of just how effective the use of props can be came about when Alan Winchester, then managing director of his own printing firm, decided to purchase more printing machinery. The problem was that the supplier coming in to meet him had been sticking to his guns on price and Alan needed to get him to move.

To achieve this, Alan set the scene with a competitor's quote on his desk and set up a 'phone call from them to come in during his meeting. The call was just for Alan to confirm that he had received their quotation.

On the day in question, the meeting began; just 20 minutes later, in came the call. Alan took the call saying "yes, I have your quotation in my hand [at this point he picked up the quotation and flicked through it], we need to decide by the end of this week, at which time I'll call and let you know our decision". This sent a number of very clear messages to the people in front of him, namely:

1. You have competition.
2. I'm deciding this week.
3. Make your decision: if you want the business, move on price.
4. This is your opportunity to get in if you want.

Creating an environment for something like this to happen can only be done for negotiations conducted on your home ground.

Remember – the tables can be turned

Real prop intimidation can be used on you as well, so keep a sharp eye out for this. Don't get confused as to your reason for being there; focus on getting the deal you want. Also, take a look at the list below of 'props' that are used against all of us every day.

- Newly decorated offices, with big plants and a reception to go with them.
- The list of big-name clients on the wall.
- Their international list of offices and affiliates.
- Parking places which say Mr _____ and his private plate.
- The welcome board with just about everybody else on it but you.
- Impressive photographs, framed with the man in question on his yacht, speedboat, racing car, and what ever else they can think of.
- Their gadgets collection.

Get off the admiration trail just for a minute and ask yourself, why do so many businesses invest in the use of props? The answer should come as a blinding flash of lightning: because they work!

CHECKLIST FOR GETTING IT RIGHT

✓ Avoid over-doing it; if they're smart they'll catch you out.
✓ Build up your own collection of props.
✓ Keep an eye out for the other side's use of props on you.
✓ Don't fall into the impression trap.

36

PERCEPTION OR REALITY? USING PERCEPTION TO YOUR ADVANTAGE

'There is no reality: only perception.'

Who first said that? There are many modern-day pundits who espouse the concept that effective reality is nothing more than what we can be made to perceive, and it may be tempting for them to believe that they discovered the concept for themselves. But it is the Greek philosopher Epictetus, born c. AD 50, who is credited with its coining.

The cornerstone of confidence

In negotiation, perception is everything. It is the corner-stone of confidence – both your own, and your opponent's. It is the result of the image you are portraying, whether or not it is the image you want. It is also the result of the image you are portraying of your product (or your interest in your opponent's product – depending upon which side of the negotiation you are). There is always a difference between the image you are intending to project and the one you perceive to be the truth. The size of that differential directly governs your own confidence in yourself.

If you make claims for yourself that you do not fully believe (and we all do!) you automatically require acting ability to persuade your opponent that you do believe them. And the more you don't believe what you are claiming, the better your acting needs to be. Human nature, and the ever-present drive for more business, will cause you to push the size of that differential to limits that become critical. At that point, you have a range of options:

1. Make the differential smaller by:

- making the true reality closer to your claims (improving the truth); or
- making your perceived reality closer to your claims (persuading yourself you have greater faith in your position); or
- reducing your claims.

2. Be a better actor.

You may think that all that is fairly obvious, and merely defines the problem, whereas what we are seeking is a solution. But there is a good reason for analysing the situation in such detail. The commonest mistake that is made in such situations is for us to be overly conscious of our own problems – our own perceptions. And the truth is that our own perceptions are not what count. It is the opponent's perceptions that matter.

However true those problems may be for you, they are just as true for your opponent.

Get out of your own head and into your opponent's

What you must do is get out of your own head, and get into your opponent's. Never make an analysis like that for yourself – only for them. The really expert negotiator is the one whose mind is sitting in the chair opposite. You should constantly home in on what you are being asked to perceive, and ask yourself why. If you cannot immediately find an answer, you may be looking at the key to the whole negotiation.

The way it works

Let's illustrate the theory by looking at the practice through the eyes of Humphrey Nelson, who recalls an occasion on which he was getting bogged down in negotiations. The company on the other side had been approached by him to supply his premises with a water-purification plant.

Humphrey, a food-ingredients manufacturer, having found a small gap in his market, had carved a sizeable market in the gap. New health and safety regulations required him to have a new form of water purification, and, because his product was very unusual, his technical requirements were equally unusual and very specific. The plant on offer was precisely correct to his specifications but the price demanded seemed exorbitant.

"I couldn't afford it, but I absolutely had to have it in order to comply with a whole new set of bylaws. They were the only people who made it, so they had me over a barrel. This was the first time I had regretted having such an esoteric product. If I had been producing something more mundane, there would have been a dozen plants that would have suited my purposes, and I could have played suppliers off against each other.

"What was particularly upsetting was that sales were fantastic, and I had been scrabbling together every penny I could find to open more premises to meet the expanding demand. This was going to push my plans back several crucial months – which could be catastrophic if it gave the emergent competition time to catch me up. You might have some idea as to how depressing the situation seemed. I began to develop a really hefty hate for the opposition!

They were as eager to sell as I was to buy

"And then I suddenly realised that I was becoming so obsessed with my position that I was overlooking something that was staring me in the face – their position. How many people were there who would need this particular type of plant? Suddenly, I realised that they were at least as eager to sell as I was to buy.

"And having 'got inside their heads', I also saw their problem with regard to the price. They had spent a lot of money on research and development in order to plug a small gap in the market (which was exactly what I had done with my product), and now they desperately needed to recoup it. In that glorious moment of enlightenment, I saw where to go.

"I simply laid my cards on the table. All of them! I even itemised my expansion plans, and explained how the cost of their equipment was going to scupper them – possibly forever, if it caused me to lose my near-monopoly share of the market.

"Seeing the opportunity to sell not one but, very soon, two or more plants, they began falling over themselves to come up with all sorts of financial proposals to help me. In no time at all we had a terrific deal. And all because I got inside their heads!"

CHECKLIST FOR GETTING IT RIGHT

✓ Perception is what matters, and their perception is more important to you than yours.
✓ The really expert negotiator is the one who mentally sits in the opposite chair.

37

THE 'NICE MAN, NASTY MAN' PLOY (OR, 'TWO AGAINST ONE' TACTIC)

'... many of us fail to appreciate when it is being used against us in business.'

Not that old trick

We have all seen the detective film or war film in which one side tries to get the other to speak using the 'nice man, nasty man' ploy. We have all, no doubt, immediately recognised the ploy and seen the folly of giving in to the nice man. After all, the nice man and the nasty man are on the same side, aren't they?

It wouldn't work with me – would it?

Strangely, while most people easily spot the technique used as entertainment, many of us fail to appreciate when it is being used against us in business. Its purpose is, of course, not only to unsettle us, but also to shift the negotiating range in the opposition's favour. We are so concerned that the negotiating decision may rest with the nasty man, or woman, that we are willing to concede ground to the nice person. We are often only too ready to believe that the nice person is actually trying his or her best for us; that he or she is indeed on our side!

We might be ready to concede to the nice person's offer because we believe it is the best position we can achieve. Nevertheless, the technique does have potential disadvantages. Skilled negotiators will always suspect it is being used against them when the other side produces two people singing different tunes. Moreover, they can turn this knowledge to their advantage, seize the moral high ground and escape the role of victim.

How can we respond?

So how should we react when the ploy is used against us? By informing the other side, politely of course, that we know what they are doing. Here is the sort of remark you could make: "You know I'm sure I would find it much easier to reach agreement with you if I felt I was negotiating to one set of criteria. As it is, I find I am talking to two different people who are adopting different positions". Of course, depending on how well you know the opposition, you might feel able to say quite simply, "Oh no, not the old nice man, nasty man ploy. Let's get beyond that shall we and down to some real business?". In our culture, it is likely that you would be quite so blatant only if there existed a tried and trusted working relationship.

Another response is to try to cut the hard person out of the negotiation. You can explain to the 'friendly' opponent that you would really like to reach a settlement but, unfortunately, the colleague is making this impossible. Much as you would regret doing so, you may have to look elsewhere to do a deal. In fact, you will do so if the other person continues to take part in the negotiation.

The reality is that you do not wish to walk away and end up with a lose-lose conclusion. Nevertheless, as you will be well aware, you should always be prepared to walk away from a negotiation. And the other side should know that you do have a bottom line, even if they do not know what that is.

The way it works
So how might the ploy work in practice? Well, consider Sarah Butler's position as head of administration in a small manufacturing company. The company makes a variety of small leather goods but concentrates on its range of handbags. Each item is presented for sale with a printed card, which varies according to the nature of the item. Consequently, the firm uses a wide range of different cards but has neither the space nor the financial resources to stock large quantities.

Sarah is anxious to agree a new contract with a printing company in the area. There are several to choose from but one of them appeals particularly to her, because it is reliable and because she has virtually reached agreement on two of her criteria: quality and cost. Delivery time is now the biggest problem. One of the partners, John Williams, has a fairly abrupt style and will not agree to any contractual arrangement about time. The other, Peter Simpson, has hinted that a maximum turnaround time of three weeks might be possible. Sarah's bottom line is two weeks but she would like to gain agreement to ten days.

Of course, the printing firm see Sarah's orders as fairly small fry but nevertheless very useful to them, particularly if they can retain flexibility on timing and use the order to smooth out their own work-flow. John and Peter have no intention of losing Sarah's order if they can possibly avoid doing so.

Foiling the ploy
Fortunately for her, Sarah recognises the ploy. She too, is keen to reach agreement but plays the reluctant buyer with Peter, explaining that John has put an agreement in jeopardy by apparently failing to appreciate the importance of timing. She may have to look elsewhere, and, of course, is prepared to do so.

Peter's response is to assure her that they can reach agreement. In fact they agree to a maximum two-week turnaround time, to their mutual advantage.

CHECKLIST FOR GETTING IT RIGHT

✓ Watch for the ploy whenever you are dealing with more than one person.
✓ Listen carefully for differences in their negotiating positions.
✓ Remember that, despite any differences, they are both on the same side.
✓ Try initially to trade one off against the other.
✓ If necessary, come clean with the nice guy and try to ditch the nasty one.
✓ Use a style and tone appropriate to the people concerned and to your relationship with them.
✓ Be polite and constructive and do not try to embarrass them overtly.
✓ As always, be prepared to walk away

'... find out where the gaps in your power lie ...'

In negotiations, it is vital to recognise when a party is using and abusing its power. You also need to recognise the different types of power available. Research by two sociologists, French and Raven, in the 1950s, identified eight types of power that can be exerted.

Eight types of power

They are:

- **Positional power.** A managing director will have power over his assistant, because of his position of authority.
- **Information power.** Knowing more about a subject than someone else makes them dependent on you when they want to have that information.
- **Reward control.** A managing director has the power to reward people for their performance. That control makes those people dependent on him.
- **Coercive power.** The power to punish people (withdraw benefits / salary, etc.) who don't perform, is a form of coercive power. It's the reverse side of the control of rewards. It makes people dependent because they depend on the punishment not being carried out.
- **Alliances and networks.** This is a device designed to increase power using both positional and information power. If you wanted to increase your own power position in relation to, say, your chief executive who is in authority over you, try to co-opt the backing of someone on a par with the chief executive. You will increase the chance of getting your ideas accepted.
- **Controlling the agenda.** This method is used to exclude items that are unfavourable to the person in control of the agenda and to include the most favourable items.
- **Control of meaning and symbols.** The way in which an office is arranged and guests greeted and arranged in a room can all be done in such a way as to exercise the maximum power and influence over the others involved.
- **Personal power.** This type of power is one that comes from admiration of the qualities that someone possesses. They may have a charismatic quality that makes people sit up and listen to what they have to say. This can have a considerable influence on other people.

Use these eight types of power to assess your strengths and weaknesses

If you are about to start a negotiation, you can assess your position against each of the types of power. It can help you find out where the gaps in your power lie, which power tactics to focus on and what information you might need to enhance your negotiating position. You also need to be aware when one or more of these power tactics is being used against you.

The way it works

Jim Meade is a sales manager who has spent several years selling to senior directors of major corporations. He explains how he once encountered a particularly difficult managing director, who used an unusual power tactic.

"I had been warned that this particular managing director was prickly. What was absurd was the way he sat in a chair behind a large leather table that elevated his position. I was invited to sit on an extremely low chair, well behind and away from his desk.

I could see the game he was trying to play

"Fortunately, I could see the game he was trying to play straight away and before I sat down, I feigned a back injury and the need for a straight upright chair which he had no option but to call for. It immediately blocked his strategy to make me feel inferior. To make a point, when the chair was brought, I took it right up to his desk asking politely if he would mind me using a corner of it. I explained that I would need to use it for part of my demonstration. Although this could have made him feel uncomfortable because I had invaded his personal space, in fact, it had the opposite effect. It brought us on to a level playing field. In spite of the barrier of the desk, I was able to build a rapport with him. He even ended up becoming one of our best customers.

"I hate to think how the story would have ended if I had not engineered myself into a more comfortable position. I am certain that I would not have felt as comfortable as I did. Without a doubt, it would have been an uphill struggle to create any confidence between us. I doubt he would have become such a good customer."

CHECKLIST FOR GETTING IT RIGHT

✓ Check your sources of power before you negotiate.
✓ Have you left any out?
✓ Know which one is the strongest.
✓ Make sure any weak spots are covered.

| 39 | **GETTING CARRIED ALONG ON THE BANDWAGON** |

'He set off to spend £400 on a printer and instead spent £3,000 on a new system.'

We all have to watch out for the dirty-tricks brigade, particularly when they create such a level of momentum in the negotiations that we get lulled into agreeing to much more in the way of concessions than we would normally. When human relationships are working well and the rapport level is high, it is easy to get carried away and agree to almost anything, particularly if the competitive angle or supply limitation principles are exploited.

The auction effect

This often occurs at auctions, where seemingly sane individuals get carried away and make much higher bids than necessary to beat the other buyers. If the item is said to be one of only a few or in short supply generally, this increases the pressure for the person to say 'yes', often to a very unfavourable deal. When questioned after making an unfavourable bid, buyers will often rationalise their emotional buying decision with apparently sound, logical arguments. Don't be fooled! The person has still been carried away by the auction effect, even if they can justify their decision with logic!

Beware the 'yes tag'

There are many ways skilled negotiators can get their opponents caught up in the momentum of the deal. One of those ways is the use of techniques such as 'yes tags', where you always follow a statement with a tag such as "don't you agree?", or "you'd like to see this system installed, wouldn't you?" and so on. The 'yes tag' approach is very effective, so watch out for it being used against you!

Feel, felt, found

Another technique often used to avoid the building of barriers to the process of moving the negotiation forward to agreement is the 'feel, felt, found' technique, which has been around for many years. It is still surprisingly effective, if used elegantly, and even its own practitioners sometimes get caught by it. The process goes something like this ...

Customer: "I'd like the economy of running a diesel car but they are noisy, smelly and they don't accelerate very quickly". Salesperson: " I know how you feel, because that's what I used to feel about driving diesel. What I've found, however, since I've been driving this one is that ...". This technique is very effective. The normal reaction of the salesperson would be to disagree with the customer after the first statement. However, if this were to happen, a barrier of disagreement would have been created and the negotiations would have ground to a halt.

85

Went to buy a printer, bought a whole computer system

Simon runs a successful architect's practice and makes full use of the latest information technology. One day, his laser printer decided to jam and he couldn't fix the problem himself. It was a manufacturer's repair job which would take three days. He could not afford to be without a printer for that time, so he despatched the broken machine to the manufacturer and headed off towards his local discount computer store, to buy another printer to act as backup if this situation ever happened again. As he walked through the store towards the printer section, he noticed the gleaming new systems displaying the latest software and smiled to himself, thinking how computers had developed since he bought his system last year.

Looking through the printers, he was unable to find a duplicate of the printer which had broken down, so he asked the advice of one of the sales people. The model he currently had was no longer available and its replacement was considerably more than he had planned to pay. However, the salesperson was so enthusiastic about the various options for the replacement printer that Simon soon found himself being shown several complete systems, each including a 'free' printer of a similar specification to the one he was seeking. About an hour later, Simon was loading a complete new system, including a sophisticated printer, into the back of his estate car. He had set off to spend £400 on a printer and ended up spending £3,000 on a new system, all because of the enthusiasm of the salesperson, who led him along a very enjoyable path of showing him the opportunities provided by the new equipment.

Simon now has the new system installed at home, with the printer available as backup in case his main one ever goes wrong again. There is no buyer remorse, because, even to this day, Simon has convinced himself that he really did need this new system, even if he hadn't realised that need when he set out to buy the additional printer. The enthusiasm of the salesperson made the store a lot of money that day!

CHECKLIST FOR GETTING IT RIGHT

✓ Beware the 'auction effect'. Check you are not getting carried away in the heat of the moment.
✓ Listen for the use of 'yes tags' and beware! They are used to create momentum for an agreement which you may regret.
✓ Watch for the use of 'feel, felt, found' in its various forms. It's persuasive.
✓ Take the 'fly on the wall' position regularly during the negotiation and ask yourself what is really happening at each stage.
✓ Check what you are now being asked to spend, compared to what you set out to spend. What additional services are being provided to account for this extra amount?
✓ If there is a 'cooling-off' period as part of the deal, take independent advice and ask yourself whether, if you could turn the clock back, you would still agree to the deal.

40 | FIGHT AGAINST THE DESIRE TO GET YOUR OWN BACK

'A good negotiation is not a battle ...'

What's wrong with making them pay?

If you have been thwarted in the past by an opponent or competitor, getting your own back will have a certain obvious attraction. In any case, negotiation is obviously a competitive business and what is wrong with a win-lose outcome, in which you are the winner?

It is true that there are occasions when a win-lose outcome in your favour is the best you can achieve, but it is certainly not the best you might have hoped for. A good negotiation is not a battle but an attempt by two sides to get maximum value from a situation. It nearly always involves a range of criteria, with each side putting different values on each criterion. This is where the scope for negotiation really lies.

Good negotiating principles

Consider the following principles of good negotiating:

- Each side shows concern for the other's objectives;
- Each sees the other as fair;
- The outcome is a win-win situation;
- Each feels they would enjoy negotiating again.

These principles do not obviate the need for hard negotiation but they do help to foster a good reputation and a sound relationship for the future. A desire for revenge is clearly incompatible with these principles, since it implies a certain level of deviousness. No opposing negotiators will want to do business with you if they know that revenge is your prime motivator.

Be constructive

Desire for revenge is an emotion best kept out of negotiations. Warmth and friendliness are also emotions but they are constructive and can, clearly, help proceedings. Vengefulness is destructive, not just of the opposition, but also of ourselves, if we choose to give it expression. It can rebound on us unexpectedly, particularly if our opponents suspect our motives and harden their approach or pull out of the negotiation altogether. Future relationships might be irretrievably damaged.

Pros and cons

Clearly, vengefulness can exact a heavy penalty from those who choose to give in to it, but what are its advantages? Well there really is only one and that is a certain self-indulgent satisfaction. You might think that a desire to get your own back will give you an added drive to succeed but, more likely, it will cloud your thinking and give an intellectual advantage to the other side. It is far better to keep your eye on the ball and concentrate on the important issues.

The way it works

Fred Jordon is the MD of an electrical engineering firm in the Midlands. They make a range of small components but concentrate on the manufacture of oscillators. Nearly three years ago, his firm had signed a contract with an office-cleaning company. At the time, Fred had stressed to Brian Williams, who negotiated the contract on the firm's behalf, that the standard working week for cleaning should include Saturday mornings. After the contract had been signed, Fred discovered that Saturday mornings had not been included. Consequently, additional cleaning hours had to be agreed at time and a half.

What can happen when the other side draws up the contract

Brian had been furious and very embarrassed, claiming that the cleaning firm had agreed during negotiations to include Saturday mornings at the standard weekly rate. Unfortunately, Brian had agreed to let the firm draw up the contract. Worse still, neither Brian nor Fred had read the small print before signing.

The issue was not one to have any significant impact on the company's finances but, now that the contract had almost expired, Brian was determined that the cleaning company should not win the contract next time! Yet, as Fred pointed out to Brian, the contract had been extremely successful.

In the subsequent tendering process, the same cleaning firm again made the most attractive submission. Fred's wiser counsel prevailed and the firm were taken on again. Subsequently, Fred learned from the cleaning company's MD that the omission of reference to Saturday mornings in the original contact had been a genuine error on their part. They had been quite content to include it in the second contract. The two firms continued to maintain a sound and constructive working relationship.

 ## CHECKLIST FOR GETTING IT RIGHT

✓ Consider if your resentment is fully justified.
✓ Were you part of the problem?
✓ What will be the tangible result of getting your own back?
✓ What do you stand to lose?
✓ If your resentment is justified and based on a significant issue, would it not be wiser simply to avoid further dealings than to seek revenge?

7 SNARES AND AMBUSHES

41 HOW TO LEAD THEM UP THE GARDEN PATH AND HAVE THEM EATING OUT OF YOUR HAND

'... you can get them to do exactly what you want ...'

Manoeuvring someone into a position in which they do exactly what you want is not difficult. All that is required is the right approach. Be careful, though, not to cause friction. It can be easy to put someone off, by trying to dominate the proceedings and bulldozing them into accepting your point of view. Such an approach will lead only to one outcome: conflict. You may persuade them to say 'yes' on the spot. Later on they will reject you.

Think the way they think

There is a very simple technique, however, that you can use to get someone eating out of your hand (ethically and legitimately) without causing offence or by making them feel that they have in some way been manipulated. What you do is phrase your sentences so they are perfectly in tune with your opposite number's way of thinking, stressing the benefits you have to offer.

Imagine you run a public relations company that specialises in obtaining radio air time. You're negotiating with a new client, who is keen to get more people into his store. The conversation could go something like this: 'It is very timely that you've approached us. We have just successfully completed a project for another local firm, Sindalls, that was very similar to this. They were delighted with the exposure they received and have reported a 20 per cent increase in traffic through their store. If I understand you correctly, your objective is to increase the flow of people through your shop at a time when it is traditionally quietest for you. Am I right in my analysis of your mission? [*check for response*] Because I know we can help you. Here's how ...'

Check regularly that you are 'in tune'

The technique used here is to check the progress of what the other party wants. Your aim is to get them to agree with you. Once that is achieved, you can move on to the next step and again, check that what you say fits in with their mission. Putting yourself in the shoes of the other person, linking the benefits to *them*, is the easiest way to get them to do what you want. If, after checking the progress of what you're suggesting they say "no, that's not right", you can check what they do want and repackage the deal so it satisfies them.

How a leading question differs from a progress question

Watch out for the distinction between asking leading questions and progress questions. A progress question is simply rephrasing what has already been said, to check meaning. Leading questions may ignore what has been said before and invite a particular response. They are designed to entrap the other person into saying something that they don't necessarily agree with. It may invoke a 'yes' response at the time, but, later on, they will feel manipulated, and you may end up having to start your negotiations over again. The net result will be a lot of wasted time and effort.

You may not always be able to find out in advance exactly what someone's needs are. You can still steer them into a position where you get them to do something for you. Not by asking any leading questions but simply by suggesting what you want in a way that gets the benefit to them across. Start off with the benefit – get them to see the advantage and then move on to a question that opens up the way for you to sell those benefits to them.

The way
it works
Using the public relations example, the PR agent could approach it like this:

"You would like to get more people visiting your shop. You don't have a prime site with a lot of people passing by, so you have to rely on word of mouth to get them to come. Using radio you can talk directly to a large proportion of the local population. Would you like to hear how it works?"

CHECKLIST FOR GETTING IT RIGHT

✓ Put yourself in the other party's shoes and ask yourself what they would like to hear.
✓ Avoid trying to dominate and bulldoze your way.
✓ Think the way they think.
✓ Use progress questions.
✓ Avoid leading questions.

42

DON'T CLOSE OFF ESCAPE ROUTES

'... *always try to have some alternatives prepared* ...'

The art of successful negotiation is constantly to seek opportunities at which both parties to the negotiation can move forward, and gain as a result of the process. There are, sometimes, occasions when we have to walk away from a deal but this should only happen after an extensive period of trying other options.

Before or after?
If you say 'no' to someone else's suggestion or proposal, it is highly likely that they will perceive your attitude as negative. They will not listen to any further comments you make as to why you have just said 'no'. A more constructive approach is first to explain your reasons why you cannot agree. By doing this, you provide them with an insight into their proposal that they may have missed and which they can then agree is a cause for concern. You may also highlight something in their proposal which is unattractive to them as well. Unless 'no' means 'no, never', always leave room to search for other options.

"We couldn't produce this quantity in the time you have stated" doesn't mean it is impossible. It means, is it possible to be more flexible on the time, or the quantity, so that we can agree to your proposal? Leaving the door open requires active listening on the part of both parties.

Alternatives
When entering into a negotiation, try to have some prepared alternatives or other options, so that you always have a fall-back position.

If you have no alternatives, you run the risk of either walking away from a deal because it is unacceptable or agreeing to a deal which is unattractive to you. Both outcomes can be avoided with a little planning. Alternatives can either be options to explore with the other party, or totally separate opportunities you may have with other parties with whom you are negotiating.

The way it works
Chris Matthews runs a large hardware business and decides to try a new, better wholesaler. The wholesaler delivers free of charge, on the understanding that deliveries are made on Wednesday afternoons. Chris cannot agree to this because Wednesday is market day in the local town and one of his busiest days. Not only is the shop busy but the car park in front of the shop is also full.

Instead of saying that he cannot agree to Wednesday deliveries, Chris puts forward his reasons first. He asks about the delivery route on Wednesdays and discovers that he will be added to an existing round that covers a large area. He explains about the market, the traffic, the lack of space in the car park, and the lack of help for the driver in unloading the lorry. He says that this is why Wednesday is out of the question. The last thing the wholesaler wants is his vehicle delayed in traffic. A compromise is sought and, for a small delivery charge, the wholesaler rearranges another route so that deliveries can be made on a Tuesday.

The alternative   A few years ago, a major company in the Far East was very keen to do business with a UK company but were not prepared to enter into the franchise arrangement that the UK company was seeking. The Far Eastern company tried every way they could to get all the commercial details of the UK company's products, without having to commit themselves to a franchise arrangement. Seeing that a franchise deal was unlikely, the UK company entered into a spot-trading arrangement with this company on part of its product range and opened negotiations with a competitor. The spot arrangements were less attractive to the UK company but it enabled them to develop closer contacts with other, more interested, parties. Eventually, the UK company stopped the spot-trading and signed a franchise agreement with one of these other companies. The original company wasn't pleased but they had been offered the deal and had turned it down.

CHECKLIST FOR GETTING IT RIGHT

✓ Actively listen to what is said.
✓ Only say 'no' when you really mean it.
✓ Always search for other options.
✓ If the business is important, always have alternatives.

43 | WHAT TO DO WHEN THEY KEEP SAYING 'BUT'

'... techniques to stop them from stringing the negotiations out.'

Turning the negative into positive

'But ...' is such a negative way to start any statement. During a negotiation, if the other side start to use 'But ...' frequently, it is a clear indicator that the negotiation style has turned negative. You need to take control of this negative atmosphere and turn it round. To achieve this, adopt a positive questioning style, which prevents them from continuing with their negative questioning style. This will:

- take control of the negotiation and steer it back in a constructive direction.
- prevent them from stringing out the negotiation and grinding you down; and
- allow you to ask structured questions and take charge of the negotiation.

How does the process work?

During the negotiation, you detect a level of negativity from the other party. You will be aware of an attitude in the other party that is reactive rather than active towards the negotiation. Most of their statements or responses will be prefaced with the word 'But ...'. There are two possible explanations for their behaviour:

- They are deliberately using 'But ...' as a negotiating tactic to throw you off balance and gain the upper hand. This approach is conscious.
- They are unsure. The real question they are asking is for you to take time to explain in more detail the advantages for them of what is proposed. This approach is unconscious.

Whichever cognitive state they are in, you can apply the same approach to turning the situation back in your favour. The key to success here is to identify their negative mode and ask a question about it, for example:

'It is no problem to go over the payment terms one more time, so that we can address them. Please, tell me, exactly what concerns do you have?'

This is a well known questioning technique, which delivers a statement under the auspices of a question. What happens is that the statement is accepted without question, because they are thinking about the answer that you have just demanded from them. You have asked the question because you have said "please, tell me". 'Tell me' is a very direct request that is softened by placing a 'please' in front of it.

By using a question such as this, you are doing three things:

1. You are acknowledging that they have a concern, which means that you are being sensitive to their needs. If they are not already aware of their concern you will have articulated it for them.

2. You are directly asking them to tell you about it.
3. You are stating that you will address any concerns they may have.

This question will prompt them to divulge their concerns. At this point, you need to be firm and use further questions to bring their concerns about the issue of payment terms, to use the above example, out into the open fully.

Do not let them wonder off on to another subject or another concern. Be firm. You must manage their concern and work through to a resolution that is acceptable both to you and to them, and then get their agreement to move on.

Repeating the process

This process manifests itself as a series of closed questioning loops. You will go round in tight circles, fixing their concerns, and then move on. The most effective part of this technique is the control that you are assuming, within the overall framework of the negotiation. They have been pursuing a negative, reactive style of negotiation. You have been pursuing a positive, active style of negotiation. When you come out of the other side of this segment of the negotiation you will be in the commanding position.

 ## CHECKLIST FOR GETTING IT RIGHT

✓ Turn the negative into positive.
✓ Ask directly about the other party's concerns and address their needs actively.
✓ Be strong – do not let them wander off the subject and back to a negative approach to the negotiation.
✓ Keep on tackling each and every concern until the negotiation is back on track.

44	## "COME ON, TRUST ME, IT'LL NEVER HAPPEN ..."

'Always ask yourself 'what happens if it does?'.'

You are in the final stages of a negotiation, and reading the small print on the contract. You reach a clause which effectively absolves the opposition of any blame or liability in the event of something going wrong, so long as they use their 'best endeavours'.

You raise a query over this, and that's when you get the title to this section ... "Come on, trust me, it'll never happen".

So you counter with the observation that, if it does, you have wasted a great deal of money; and they reply that this is the standard contract they've used for many years and hundreds of deals, and that clause is there only to cover their backs in the event of a disaster and that 'they would look after you'.

That's all right, isn't it? You can merrily shake their hand, sign on the dotted line, pay the money and sleep easily. End of story.

If only it were that easy! The principal question you should be asking yourself is: who has more to lose – they or you?

Watch the small print
Companies include the small print in their contracts (and small print tends to be the area where this sort of question arises) for various reasons – not all of them bad. There are plenty of unscrupulous people who will use any unfair and underhand trick to get what they can out of a hapless supplier. So, the supplier has to protect itself. (In practice, it's the supplier's insurance company that will insert most of these difficult clauses in the small print.) Let us assume that you are not an unscrupulous person, and have no intention of using an unfair trick. Nevertheless, the contract you sign will be the same as if you were. Moreover, there are bad reasons for these small-print clauses. The supplier could be unscrupulous, wanting to use unfair tricks of their own.

Who has more to lose?
So we come back to that question: who has more to lose – they or you? Who is your proposed supplier? A household-name corporation with a big reputation to be damaged or a back-street, cut-price merchant with no reputation at all? Careful! Even with that apparently obvious choice, the answer is not simple. The big corporation may have sold thousands of these products, and, if they made a concession to you in the event of something going wrong that their terms of business expressly excluded from being their liability, the precedent could expose them to a gigantic compensation bill (they could also be in breach of the terms of their insurance, though that is not your problem). On the other hand, the back-

street, cut-price merchant (unless he is simply a crook) could well be trying to establish a reputation for customer care – everyone started small once.

Big or small, every legitimate business is concerned with a reputation for customer care in the current tough world. So will they look after you?

If the supplier is a big corporation, and their agent is uttering assurances, take another look at the small print. Does it have a clause expressly excluding the authority of any agent to vary the terms of the contract? If so, any negotiation is a waste of time, because the agent's assurances are meaningless (and the corporation might appreciate being told that they are being offered). If it does not have that clause, and the agent is prepared to endorse the contract with a signed, hand-written rider, varying the terms, you might be all right (though you should seek legal advice).

Can you afford the down side? If the supplier is a small operation, first of all you need to be a good judge of character. If this is not someone you feel you can trust, forget it. Even if you can trust them, what if they go out of business? If they cannot raise a warranty backed by a reputable insurance company, you have to decide whether any saving in purchase price warrants the risk, and whether you are prepared to afford the worst-case scenario.

None of this sounds much like negotiation. Let us leave the last word to my friend Christopher. He is the chairman and chief executive of a highly successful plc. Upon being shown the title of the section, his reaction was instant.

"Forget it! Don't touch it! It's those words 'Trust me'. Anyone who uses those particular words, can't be trusted. Now if they had said, 'I see your problem. Let me look into a special warranty agreement to cover that point, even if it costs a little more ...' then I'd have gone on talking to them."

 ## CHECKLIST FOR GETTING IT RIGHT

✓ Do not be swayed by 'It'll never happen': Murphy's Law says it will.
✓ If there is an offer to vary the terms of the contract, check that this is valid.
✓ Check that any warranty is securely founded.
✓ If all else fails, ask yourself if you are prepared to be your own insurer (i.e. any saving in purchase price represents the premium; can you stand the loss?)

45 DON'T BE FOOLED BY MR NICE GUY

'Mr Nice Guy can make you feel as though you are negotiating against yourself.'

By definition, nice people do not indulge in dirty negotiating tactics. Which is why successful dirty negotiators take pains to come across as affable, friendly, responsible people, who simply want to get a deal that works for both of you. Of course, many negotiators are genuinely nice people. But they are negotiators nevertheless, and, if they are worth their salt, they will not let their niceness get in the way of competent negotiating.

Watch your guard

The risk you run when faced with a nice person is that you relax your guard. Someone who enquires about your new-born daughter doesn't seem as though they are going to be all that tough. Someone who says "After you" and "What would be convenient for you?" doesn't sound as though they are going to be unreasonable. Someone who seems to like you, is relaxed in your presence and treats you as an equal doesn't give the impression that they distrust you.

You can be lulled into thinking that the negotiation will run smoothly and quickly and the outcome will be a fair and equitable one.

But Mr Nice Guys have not abandoned all the accepted techniques of negotiating. They will have studied you and your needs. They will have worked out the most persuasive arguments. They will have decided which tactics are most likely to achieve the desired effect and will use them.

How likeable are they?

Be very alert to the danger of liking someone too much. If you heave a sigh of relief after your first encounter with your opponent, if you look forward to the next meeting, if you find yourself thinking "this is someone I can definitely do business with", warning bells should be ringing.

Don't let their charm and grace go to your head

The dangers are, firstly, that you will not bother to prepare properly. Part of the preparation for any negotiation is to try to find out a bit about your opponent. A good way of doing this is to ring him or her up beforehand, to confirm the arrangements. Drop some pleasantries into the conversation and ask if there is anything that he or she would like clarified before the meeting. Someone who is going to play the Mr Nice Guy game will seize on this opportunity to stress how much you have in common and how pleasant the negotiation is going to be.

In fact, any indication you get that your opposite number is a thoroughly good egg should spur you on to better preparation and a sharper focus on what it is you want to get out of the negotiation.

98

Secondly, your alertness to various tactics will be blunted. The 'cupboard is bare' ploy or the change of mind will be delivered with such charm and grace that you could easily fall for them before recognising them for what they are. And when you do call their bluff, you will be utterly disarmed by apologies, explanations and embarrassment. You will find it very difficult to believe that they mean to mislead, misinform and manipulate. You will also run the risk of not challenging them enough and of forgiving them too easily.

Don't soften your stance

Thirdly, and most dangerously, you will want to please Mr Nice Guys. You will not want to disappoint or irritate them. You will not want to appear churlish or ungenerous next to them. It is very tempting to soften your stance and change your mind about what you are and are not prepared to accept. You may have no problem with screwing a supplier down to the last penny on a bulk deal but this is different. This man has children the same age as yours. He has let on that he shares the same concerns as you about schooling, about the future, about mortgage interest rates. Nice Guys can make it feel as though you are negotiating against yourself. There is no way you can reasonably ask them to throw in delivery and returned stock replacement free of charge – can you?

The Nice Guy, genuine or otherwise, is one of the most difficult types to negotiate against. You must be doubly alert to the tactics being used against you and to your own internal pressures, which will lead you to make mistakes.

CHECKLIST FOR GETTING IT RIGHT

✓ Take niceness to be a warning sign.
✓ Re-double your efforts in preparing for negotiation.
✓ Give yourself regular pep-talks about sticking to your guns.
✓ Be extra alert for all the usual negotiating ploys and recognise them for what they are.
✓ Do not make excuses in your mind for Mr Nice Guy.

'... that is simply not so.'

"More coffee?" *No, thanks I'm fine* "OK. Let's get down to business. I have two other suppliers to see and the deadline for the project is really pressing. I want to investigate the increase in productivity we can get first; we would certainly want a 10 per cent rise, so perhaps you could lay out the details of how you could secure such a figure." *Well, that's a high figure, but let's see ...*

You know the feeling. The offer of coffee was probably genuine – the pot was on the table – but the speaker has no intention of seeing two other suppliers, certainly not at short notice, as the project timing is not at this stage under any pressure. And 10 per cent? Well, it is a nice round figure ...

Confidence and credibility

If you say anything with a sufficient degree of confidence, there is a good chance that it will be believed; especially if it said from a position of authority or negotiating power. So, take everything with a pinch of salt and you will be safe from those who would tell you black was white if it gave them an edge *and they thought they could make you believe it.*

Sometimes what you are told will be just plain wrong; perhaps in the conversation above 5 per cent would be a good result, for example. Or it will be confusing. Many ways exist to state something in a way that makes people take a particular message, though it is not quite the full truth. For example, people will:

- Use an estimate as if it is an exact figure;
- Quote a figure to several places of decimals, when it is still an estimate;
- Concentrate on one issue, blinding you with facts in order to submerge everything else and obscure the omission of key information about something else;
- Drop a crucial word into the conversation, positioned and emphasised to let you ignore it. Watch for words and phrases like: if...; let's assume ...; basing it on ...

What response?

There is certainly no one 'magic formula' for avoiding intended misinformation. But some things are clear. You can:

- Make it clear that you give attention to detail: "I've looked at the figures very carefully, we have to get this absolutely right...";
- Check from time to time what you are being told: "Let me be sure I've got this right, you say the project will take three and half weeks";
- Make notes: "Just let me note that down, we will no doubt need to refer to it later ...";
- Query what is said: "That seems unlikely, are you sure ...?".

All the above will make it less likely that anyone will try such a ploy on you again.

100

It is likely to help if you think about an impending negotiation in terms of those issues on which someone would most benefit from feeding you misinformation. They are, after all, less likely to risk being caught out over minor matters.

Caught in the act

What about when you spot someone misrepresenting the facts? There are really two main options:

1. Use it without revealing it

It could be useful to you to let the confusion run, or at least to do so for a while. Wily negotiators take some pleasure in watching a less-experienced opponent digging the hole he is in deeper. Misinformation, just like the lies it really is, is difficult to sustain. You may spot that something is wrong, then see the 'fact' fail to match up with something else; and then go for the kill "How can you say that? If what you said about ... earlier is true, then both can't be right. Are you trying to catch me out?".

2. Question it at once

If you really feel that to have something unclear (to be charitable about it) on the table, as it were, is simply putting the whole process at risk, it is better to say so: "That is simply not so". Clearly, the more you come on strong, the more certain you have to be of your own facts. However, an unmasked piece of misinformation may strengthen your case.

Overall, this is an aspect of negotiation about which you should keep your guard up – throughout the process. More so, if there is a strong basis for doubting the goodwill of the other side.

CHECKLIST FOR GETTING IT RIGHT

✓ Get your own facts right.
✓ Act to minimise the likelihood of being deceived.
✓ Check where necessary.
✓ Expose where this is to your advantage.

8 | GAINING THE EDGE

47 | DIVIDE THE OPPOSITION, SO YOU CAN CONQUER

'Cause division in their camp, so you can be the peace-maker'

Tactic 70 discussed the importance of asking questions, in order to find out more about the opposition, their likes and dislikes and the type of people they are, as well as their specific requirements for this deal. But all of that assumed that we were dealing one-to-one with a single representative of the prospect company.

What if we are dealing with more than one? On the face of it, it would appear as if the techniques concerning small-talk are immediately neutralised. After all, though you can break the ice with an individual by talking about their latest skiing holiday, it is not so simple if there are six people facing you.

The principle of asking questions is still the same

However, up to a point, you can still apply the same principle, as long as you address a topic which is common to all of them. Therefore, unless you happen to learn that they all went skiing together, you'd best avoid the subject. In smalltalk terms, you're restricted to commenting on their office building (its view, the reception area, etc.), the weather, the Test Match score, any sensational news-story which you might have heard on your car radio on the way there and which they might not yet have heard, etc. It is a lot more difficult to do, the field is much narrower and, unless you happen quickly to strike gold with a particular topic, you should keep it short and always have your antennae out for anyone there who is not a bit interested in the subject. However, the principle of asking questions remains the same: ("Has anyone heard what Atherton's reached?" is better than "Guess what the score is!", because they would rather bask in the glory of purveying information than be seen to be updated by you.

When the subject gets around to business, the field really opens up to an extent that more than compensates for the lack of small-talk options. Why should the other party choose to be represented by so many people? Lift your eyes from the page for a moment, and consider that question ...

The chances are that you have homed in on the necessity to have different areas of expertise represented – technical, financial, legal, etc. – and I agree with you. But the important point here is that different areas of expertise also means different interests. They would not bother to include, for instance, a legal expert, unless they perceived a danger that the technical expert would fly off on his own hobby horse without proper attention to the legalities. And the same goes for all the other areas of expertise represented. They are all there to fight their respective corners.

In other words, before you open your mouth – or even before you walk in – there is potential for conflict between the representatives of your opposition. Isn't that beautiful?

Find where areas of negotiation are most sensitive

All you have to do, therefore, is find where areas of negotiation are most sensitive for the people involved, and then amplify the differences between the members of the opposite team – or rather, arrange for them to amplify themselves. This last point is most important, because you should not be seen to be stirring up trouble. It all comes down – once again – to your asking the right questions: "Are you chiefly concerned with the quality of the system, or the cost?".

Do you need any more examples? Simply by asking for a priority value-judgement between issues that represent the respective responsibilities of two team-members, you expose a potential conflict of interest.

They may well reply by saying that the two are equally important, but they don't believe it. By periodically introducing an area of concern to each of the personnel present, you raise the spectre of that interest conflicting with others. All the time that you are doing it, you should be earnest and sincere in your understanding of the points made by the different parties. After a while, if you've conducted the campaign sensitively, without ever voicing your opinion but merely asking theirs, you will be seen by each of them as their personal ally. In the event of two of them actively disagreeing with each other, you have the chance to be the peace-broker – paraphrasing in a most reasonable fashion the points each is making, and understanding both.

You can marshal the arguments in your favour

All the time, because you are hardly speaking, you have the chance to marshal the necessary arguments in support of your product to satisfy their various wants. When you come to lay the arguments before the assembly, they should all be on your side.

Eric Brewster runs team-building courses for executives. He says, "If all the people running departments within companies were less possessive about their own kingdoms, I'd be out of a job". I rest my case.

CHECKLIST FOR GETTING IT RIGHT

✓ Keep asking questions.
✓ With those questions, keep exposing different priorities within the opposing team.
✓ Let them have their disagreements, but always be seen to understand all sides.
✓ When the moment is right, present your case in such a way as to be seen to have solved all their problems.

48 | SALAMI-SLICE NEGOTIATIONS

'... a useful technique to slow down the pace of a negotiation ...'

Have you ever entered into a negotiation that you thought would take you no more than a week to sort out and you suddenly find that three months have slipped by and you are still without an agreement? The chances are the opposition have used the salami-slice technique on you.

It can be frustrating if you are in a hurry

It is a useful technique to slow down the pace of a negotiation but, if you are anxious to get an agreement signed, it can be frustrating in the extreme. How is this achieved? Salami comes in nice, thin slices. What the salami negotiator does is take the negotiation slice by slice. It is a technique favoured by teams of lawyers who enjoy poring over a contract into the night. What they do is question every clause, debate the phrasing of every sentence and, in some cases, individual words. The contract gets sliced into tiny pieces. The technique can be used on any agreement in which there is a lot of 'small-print' that needs to be examined.

Understand their goals

The goal of the salami negotiator is not always easy to determine. Do they have genuine concerns about the agreement or are they keen to drag the negotiations out for as long as possible? Or, are they stalling because they have decided they don't want to reach an agreement after all, but don't want to lose face by withdrawing from it just yet?

Use the counter-demand technique

What can you do if you suspect you are being salami-sliced? If you are not in a hurry to reach an agreement, one approach can be to retaliate with your own salami-slices. For each demand they make to change the agreement, you put in a counter-demand for two changes. They will soon grow tired of slicing salami and will look instead for bigger chunks to deal with.

Set a timetable

If you suspect the technique is being applied either because they want to drag their feet or because they don't want to reach a proper agreement, set a reasonable and realistic timetable for the negotiations. Tell them that if an agreement is not reached by the end of June and contracts signed by the end of July you will have no alternative but to break off negotiations and go elsewhere. You will soon determine if they are sincere or only half-hearted.

The way it works

Jim Lowe runs a successful insurance broking business. "A few years ago, we had an approach from another brokerage to buy the business. I was not looking to sell at that time but the price they were talking about was too good to miss. It was when everyone was falling over themselves to buy up whatever they could at crazy prices.

"We started the negotiations at the beginning of April. By September I started to have my doubts about the seriousness of their intention to go ahead. At the start of each meeting they were reassuring enough about their intention to proceed but they had just a couple more minor concerns. Each time it was something new. It reached the stage where every time they called I wondered what the next thing was going to be. In retrospect I should have blown the whistle much earlier but the kind of deal they were offering was too good an opportunity to let go. You always think the deal is just around the corner and if only this next hurdle can be overcome then it will happen.

Blow the whistle early if you have to

"I learned later what their strategy was. They went in with an incredibly attractive offer – enough to get you talking seriously. They would then pore over the business and look for faults. They were salami-slicing the negotiations – needling away at the price with each fault so they could try and push it down to the lowest level you would accept. For those who had become sucked into the idea of selling, it may have worked. Fortunately for us, we saw through it before a deal was agreed. If they had come to us with the price that was finally on the table we would never have entered into the negotiations in the first place. When you are in the middle of it all, it is quite hard to see what's happening. Fortunately we did, just in the nick of time."

CHECKLIST FOR GETTING IT RIGHT

✓ Are their concerns genuine or are they nit-picking?
✓ Make two demands for each one of theirs.
✓ If you are in a hurry, set a reasonable timetable.
✓ Be prepared to blow the negotiation out of the water.

49 | USING THE INFLUENCE OF PRECEDENT

'Look at what has been agreed before, or what has happened before, and use it to your advantage.'

Appealing to precedent can stop a negotiator in his or her tracks and it is a difficult tactic to combat successfully. So, if you have precedent on your side, always, always use it. And if you don't have any precedent to appeal to, try to invent some.

Where do you find precedent?

1. **Written agreement.** Any contracts or written agreements between you which contain statements of how something is done are rock-solid precedents. Don't overlook letters, faxes, memos and e-mail that has passed between your two companies in the course of everyday business. Part of the preparation for any negotiation should be the rooting out of written precedent. As well as calling on it yourself, you don't want any nasty surprises when the other side produces precedents to their advantage.

2. **De facto.** If something has been done a certain way for some time (or even only once) in the past, you can claim it as precedent. Although it was never part of the original agreement, you always found Saturday deliveries convenient and the other side accepted requests for delivery on Saturday with no complaint. This is precedent. The other side may once have agreed to a request for early settlement of one of your invoices. They did it once, they can do it again. Use it as precedent.

3. **Spurious.** Sometimes you can conjure up precedent from thin air. "We know that you would have delivered on Saturdays last year if we had asked. After all, you make Saturday deliveries to Smith & Co. next door. This is no big deal for you: you have been doing it for years."

4. **Intentional.** This is where you claim that it was always intended for some arrangement to happen, even if, in reality, it never did; that is, it was always in the spirit of the original agreement. "It has always been part of the agreement that you would deliver as often as we needed you to. Last year, we were very successful in trying to limit our demands on you to three deliveries a week. We did all we could to make things as easy as possible for you. This year, however, we need at least five deliveries a week, which is, of course, well within the terms of the agreement."

5. **Industry standard.** While the arrangement may never have been agreed or been put into effect between your two companies, appealing to an industry standard is definitely worth a try.

An example of this is a printer who, although for the last year or so had been delivering brochures exactly to order, began becoming more erratic in deliveries. Sometimes 950 brochures arrived when 1000 had been ordered, sometimes 1095 were packed in a box that was labelled as containing 1000. When the customer complained that this was unsatisfactory and not part of the original agreement, the printer replied that a 10% variation was considered acceptable and normal throughout the industry. While he would try to be more accurate, he had no obligation to be.

How do you use precedent?

1. **We have always done it this way and we don't want to change.** This is often all it takes. The power of precedent is such that many negotiators find it impossible to argue with.

2. **We can't change.** The precedent was established with good reason. The nature of your business and the whole way things operate rely on this way of doing things with your supplier.

3. **Are you reneging?** This is a more challenging use of precedent. The implication is that the other side are being less than honest in trying to ignore precedent.

4. **Are you trying to move the goal posts?** This is an outright challenge. Your rejection of any change in precedent is along the lines of "if you are going to change the precedent we might as well open a brand-new negotiation with someone else".

How do you combat an appeal to precedent?

It is not easy and you are by no means guaranteed to win every time. But try these:

1. **This is a unique negotiation.** Claim that this negotiation has nothing to do with the past and the agreement must stand on its merits, as agreed here and now. A weak opposition might crumble if you are determined enough with this argument.

2. **Times change.** Point out that the precedent is an anachronism. It is not reasonable to appeal to something which is obviously out of date.

3. **We can give you something better than precedent.** In reality, the other side have won if you try this one. They have won a concession from you. However, if you can make the concession unimportant enough from your point of view, it may well be worth it to establish that precedents can be challenged.

4. **Fixed term.** Claim that the activity under discussion was for a fixed term and never constituted a precedent. In future agreements, you may wish to insert a phrase that confirms that certain agreements are not to be taken as precedents.

CHECKLIST FOR GETTING IT RIGHT

✓ If you have precedent on your side, always, always use it.
✓ If you don't have it, invent it!
✓ Decide how you want to use it: to challenge outright or to stop them in their tracks?
✓ If it's used against you, try the techniques to combat it.

50 GRANT A CONCESSION, BUT ASK FOR AN EVEN BIGGER ONE IN RETURN

'... if we are doing that, then surely it makes best sense to ...'

Trading concessions is the core of the negotiating process. It consists of assembling, assessing and exchanging the 'variables', so as to produce a mutually acceptable deal; yet one which you still feel is good – perhaps the best – for you! Thus, accepting a concession is hardly an independent tactic, rather it is a part of the core process.

However, if you accept something, perhaps something you really want, even if a swap of some sort is involved, you may well feel you have achieved something. It can be tempting to relax and go on to the next point. But there is sometimes an opportunity here to take things further.

Minimise worth   Rarely should a concession ever be welcomed at its true worth to you, much less labelled as worth its weight in gold. If a concession's worth can be made to look insubstantial, you can, perhaps, imply that more is necessary if a fair balance is to be struck. In this way, accepting one concession can literally be used to prompt another. This is especially true if there is a logical link between the two concessions, as this makes refuting the suggestion that much harder.

So start by being grudging: "Well, I suppose that's all right. If you want this, it's not important on my side". Then move promptly into suggesting and agreeing something else. This can be linked strongly: "If we are doing that, then surely it makes best sense to ..." or just taken as read. Either way your total package may be increased.

Making it work   Like many people running a small business, James Ford is very conscious of costs. He runs a graphic-design business and it is growing. He has persuaded his accountant to spend time with him reviewing the state of the business and his plans for development; in return, he will redesign the accountant's ancient and old-fashioned letterhead. While this is the classic "if you ... then I'll ..." exchange, the balance is not quite equal and James has accepted a concession: "If it would help I can come to your office, so that you don't have any travel time" said Julia Green, who is the partner who handles his business, and he agreed, though dismissing it as no great advantage: "Fine, but I don't really mind which way round it is. Are you sure that suits?".

Julia sees it as an easy enough concession to give, after all she has other clients nearby, so she insists: "No, really, the whole arrangement is fairer that way". James shrugs, not suggesting it is in any way really helpful. Then a thought seems to strike him. "If you are to come here" he says "can you bring that software package we were discussing and then you can spend a few minutes running through it with our accounts head. I know he would appreciate it and we've been meaning to get it in for ages".

One concession leads to another Julia can think of no rapid response to refute this logic and agrees: "OK. I'll bring it, but make sure Martin's clear and ready, I can't add on too much time for this". James is quietly pleased with himself. The short demo *will* only take a few minutes, but a separate visit would otherwise have been necessary (or Martin would have had to go to the accountant's office; it will be more useful to demonstrate on their own machine). Furthermore, if this point had been dealt with separately, he would doubtless have been charged some fees, and so he has saved money and time by using one concession to lead to another.

CHECKLIST FOR GETTING IT RIGHT

✓ Accept concessions grudgingly and minimise their value to you.
✓ Look for opportunities to link – sometimes horse-and-cart-style – one concession to another.
✓ Minimise the value of the extra concession to you ("you are not doing me a big favour") and suggest it really should not be a problem to the other party either.

51 | "BUT THE CUPBOARD IS BARE"

'I'm sorry, we only have this much left in our budget.'

When you've set yourself a final figure you're prepared to pay – whether it's in a buying situation or a salary negotiation – you must then be ready to stick to it. If, after a period of negotiation, the other person isn't inclined to talk about reducing their price expectations, there's only one phrase left to utter: "I'm sorry, we only have this much left in our budget".

Don't expect negotiations to stop

This may not stop the other person trying to push you for more – or offering to wait until new budgets are allocated. If you really don't think it's worth paying any more, stand firm and say there's no deal unless they come down to your price. Now the ball's in their court.

They can either walk away or they can change the tack of their negotiations. So be prepared for the bargaining to move on to a new stage. Perhaps they will try selling you a lower cost item at the price you suggest – or a smaller amount. Only you can decide whether the new proposition is acceptable. If the suggestion is very different, you may want to begin negotiations all over again.

But be on your guard: if you say you only have a set figure left and then you agree to pay more, your word will then be doubted in all other aspects of the negotiation. And if you deal with these people again, they will never accept your final offer as final.

The way it works

"It's always a good idea to work out, in detail, exactly how much you can afford to pay and how much you think the item's worth" says Sandra Walsh, who's a buyer for a multi-national chain store. "Then, when you get to the negotiating table, you don't get carried away with the pace of the buying and overstep your limits.

"By past experience, I've found that telling someone: 'I'm not prepared to offer more for that item' is like a red rag to a bull. They either take offence and want to know what's wrong with their goods – and you lose a co-operative contact. Or they try even harder to get you to pay more, by telling you what good value you're getting and how much it'll save you in the future. It's all time-consuming and unnecessary, when you're determined you've reached your limit.

"So I just tell them my final figure and say that's all I have left in the budget for that item – which is true. That is the figure I've allocated in the budget – the rest is for other goods. That way, no one's offended."

Sometimes it works!

Sandra says sometimes the ploy works and she gets the goods at the price she's set. At other times, a whole new negotiation begins.

111

"What I do have to be on my guard for, is the counter-offer that appears similar to the original but is actually a totally different proposition. They might offer me lower-quality goods at the price I'm suggesting; or larger quantities at a lower cost per item; fewer items for my money – any combination. I categorically refuse. This is a whole new negotiation and I need to make sure I know what I'm being offered and then work out my final price on this new deal.

Don't give them cause to doubt your word

"When I first started, I was taken in by this ploy – but never again! When I say there are limited funds left in the budget, I stick to that figure. If I don't, those people will never believe me again when I make a final offer – they will always try to get me to pay more.

"If I give any concession, I show why I gave it. For example, if I agree to arrange transport, it's only because my driver was passing that way anyway. Or if I place another order at the same time, it's because that money was already allocated. I never back down on that final price."

CHECKLIST FOR GETTING IT RIGHT

✓ Decide in advance what you can afford.
✓ Hold to this as a fallback price, if the other side refuses to negotiate.
✓ Declare this is all you have to spend and stick to it.
✓ Don't expect the negotiations to stop there – they'll offer alternatives.
✓ Treat all new offers as a fresh negotiation.
✓ Guard against appearing to break your word when making concessions.

52 | PLAYING YOUR TRUMP CARD

'It gives you the initiative and helps you clinch the deal.'

A trump card

How and when to play your trump card is very important but, first, you must have a trump card and recognise it as such. A trump card is a negotiating concession of value but it must be valuable to your opponent, not necessarily to you.

Stages of negotiation

To place the trump card in context, it is useful to remind yourself of the three fundamental stages of negotiation:

- **Establish your aims.** What is your key aim(s)? What relative values do you place on them? What is your bottom line? What is your negotiating range?

- **Get information about the opposition.** Try to answer the above questions from your opponent's perspective and glean as much additional, relevant information as possible.

- **Reach for compromise.** Try to give them what they value and you do not, and to gain what you value and they do not. However, there will be issues which are important to both sides.

Think about the value

You should now know what is valuable to your opponent but you will, obviously, not give this away easily. Timing is very important to achieve maximum benefit.

In the negotiating process, it is usually good policy to make an initial low offer, below the base of your negotiating range. The offer may be ridiculed but the ridicule itself is often simply a ploy and remaining calm and unemotional is an appropriate response. Once the other side has made a concession, you can make a 'reasonable' response in reply. Your opponent will inevitably feel optimistic that progress is being made and perhaps even a little pleased with his or her own success.

Reducing their room for manoeuvring

Future concessions you make must be on a decreasingly small scale so that your opponent senses there is less and less room for manoeuvre. Hint at, but withhold, your trump card. For example, you would very much like to meet your opponent's extremely tight timescale but the possibility of doing so is extremely small. For one thing, your boss simply would not agree to it.

Your opponent will press you but you continue to resist. Clearly, you are reluctant even to speculate about it but do so only because it is clearly important to your opponent. "I really cannot see how we can possibly meet your timescale, because it would make a considerable impact on some of our other contracts" might be a suitable approach. You can then play a 'what-if' game. What would your opponent offer in return, in the unlikely event that you could meet the timescale? Since the proposition is still hypothetical, your opponent might well over-reach at this point and give an important, albeit hypothetical, concession.

Playing your trump card

When all other components of your negotiating stance are in place, play your trump card. Changed circumstances surprisingly allow you to meet the timescale, provided, of course, that the concession proposed by your opponent is still on the table. You must now aim to reach a speedy conclusion and seal the agreement. Having played your trump card, you have nothing more to offer of any significance.

Playing your trump card in this way should give you the initiative and, hopefully, clinch the deal. Your opponent will be put off his or her stride and, in case you should change your mind, will want to finalise matters immediately. You can suggest that this is a 'now or never' opportunity.

Get the timing right

Timing is, obviously, very important. If you make the offer too soon, you may lose the initiative over subsequent issues. If you stall too long, your opponent might make a deal elsewhere.

The way it works

Charles Winter runs a small business in Thetford, buying engineering fasteners overseas and selling them in the United Kingdom. One of his suppliers in Germany was anxious to sell a new device in bulk. Charles was convinced that it was just the sort of item he could sell easily and therefore wanted to buy in bulk. Nevertheless he appeared to baulk at the quantities being mentioned. He would not be able to sell them all, he said. He would be left with large numbers on the shelves. It was too big a risk.

"I really cannot see how I can buy in these numbers but, in the unlikely event that I took such a risk, how could you help me?" What would be your best price? Of course eventually, and with extreme reluctance, Charles signed to accept a large order at a relatively low price.

CHECKLIST FOR GETTING IT RIGHT

✓ Identify a key objective of your opponent which you know you can satisfy.
✓ Explain early in the negotiations that you cannot satisfy it.
✓ Show some reluctance even to discuss the matter.
✓ Gain a major hypothetical concession, in the unlikely event that you do fulfil your opponent's wishes.
✓ Try to gain agreement to all your remaining objectives.
✓ Play your trump card.
✓ Finalise the negotiation as quickly as possible.

53 | GO WITH YOUR INSTINCTS

'Listen to your still, silent voice.'

There are times in life when, despite the warnings of our inner voices, we proceed with an action. Yet we seem to know that the action is wrong and that we are making a mistake of some kind, even as we proceed.

In negotiations, one of the most useful, if not the most useful, tools at our disposal is our instinct to know when something is wrong and when something is right. We have all heard stories of people knowing when danger was approaching, knowing when to call home, knowing when to avoid taking action.

Some years ago, I heard a story of an explorer who spent sometime in the company of a group of Eskimos. One day, during their travels across an ice floe, the group had stopped to rest. The explorer decided to walk around whilst some of the group prepared a meal. Suddenly, the Eskimo leader shouted to the explorer to stand still, as there was danger just ahead of him. When the Eskimo leader reached the explorer, who had been some 100 yards away, the Eskimo explained that, just in front of where the explorer was standing, the ice was thin and above a sheer drop of over 100 feet into the icy waters below. Sure enough, when the ice was broken, the explorer found that he had indeed been standing on the edge of a precipice. How did the Eskimo Leader know for a fact that the ice was thin, as he couldn't have seen the exact spot from over 100 yards away? The only explanation the explorer put forward in his story was . . . instinct !

Tapping into the subconscious mind

It is said of humans that we have total memory, that is, we have the ability to memorise everything that happens throughout our lives. The problems we experience in the area of data are not in our memory, they are in our recall and, more specifically, being able to recall what we want, when we want it. The research of Dr Sperry, a Nobel prize-winner, certainly indicates that our memory is total.

In conversation with another person, we tend to concentrate our conscious mind on the content of what the other has said. Unless we have been trained we miss, consciously, much of the communication process, including such things as the tones of voices being used, the body-language gestures that accompany the words and the intent behind the words. However our subconscious minds do *not* miss this information. It is stored, simply waiting for us to access it.

The easiest way to access the data in our subconscious minds is ... self questioning. As a negotiation conversation proceeds ask yourself such questions as:

- "Why did they say that ?"

- "What was the intent behind that question?"
- "Why did they fold their arms then?"
- "What did that gesture mean?"
- "Why did they lower their voice just then?"
- "Was that question really for me or for the others in the room?"
- "Why did their volume of speech increase for those words?"

Look for the heart of the matter

If a negotiation is not going as you would wish, if it all seems too easy or for whatever reason you feel that something is just not quite right, take a break. Sit on your own somewhere quiet and write a question at the top of a blank sheet of paper, along the lines of "Why does this situation feel wrong ?" or "What are my feelings about this negotiation" or "Why do I feel like this ?". Then write down whatever your mind tells you. Keep writing until you cannot think of anything else to write. Within those answers to the question you have written will be an insight, a thought, an idea of whatever is troubling you.

Your mind knows you better than anyone else could possibly do. Relying on our minds to provide answers is perhaps one of the most under-utilised tools at our disposal.When you get into the habit of self questioning I believe that you will be amazed by the answers your mind will provide. However, be careful not to become paranoid, questioning every action everyone takes.

Whenever I have a problem or challenge in business and I am unsure as to the next course of action, this is how I handle it: self questioning, on paper. I am certain that you will derive great benefit from this idea.

CHECKLIST FOR GETTING IT RIGHT

✓ Listen to your inner voice.
✓ Access your subconscious mind by self questioning.
✓ You know you better than anyone else.
✓ If it feels wrong ... it probably is.

'... provide an incentive to stick to the agreement.'

In most negotiations the agreement reached between two parties is intended to be binding and is. Both parties sign up to it and both benefit from it. Just occasionally, there is a need to build into the agreement a mechanism by which, if the other party does not implement the agreement in the way set out, you can get them to see the error of their ways.

Gain a good reputation

Make sure your word is your bond. Establish a reputation for commitment and seeing agreements through, even if sometimes it means that you have to suffer a short-term disadvantage. If you don't show commitment, why should they? Be open and honest in your dealings and you will very quickly earn a reputation that will encourage others to stick the agreement they have signed up to.

If you are the lead negotiator, make sure that you have the clear authority to sign the agreement. If you don't have it, get it. This avoids the problem of agreeing to the spirit of the agreement and then having someone else try to change it.

Can they see the benefits to them?

Make sure that they not only see the benefits to them of what they are signing but that they experience some benefits quickly. This stops any backsliding and gives them a strong incentive to continue implementing their side of the bargain. If they can see immediate results they will have less desire to renege on the deal.

Show your enthusiasm for the deal by your actions, your voice and your own commitment. Enthusiasm is catching. It rubs off on others. If you are positive about the benefits of the deal to both of you, so will they be.

Let them 'own' the agreement

Where your agreement involves an element of performance, get them involved in setting their own performance targets. These might be output, quality measures, level of orders, delivery times or service levels. When the other side has come up with their suggestions, negotiate them. If you involve them in this way, they are more likely to stick to those aspects of the agreement.

Make them earn some of what they want over a period of time. As each milestone is successfully passed, so a new level of benefit is gained. This provides an incentive to stick to the agreement. It also means that you are able to reduce the benefits, should they fail to earn them.

Create dependency

Build into your agreement factors which, once agreed to, tie the other party closely to you. Once they have become more closely associated with you in the market place, the boardroom, the shop floor, or wherever, it will be more difficult for them to find positive ways of distancing themselves from you. If they try, it is likely to cause considerable disruption to their own commercial or personal objectives.

Build into the agreement severe penalties for failure to meet agreed levels of performance. These must be penalties which are meaningful and that you can enforce. If you can't implement the threat, don't make it. Having to threaten people in order to get them to stick to an agreement suggest two things.

1. It was a bad agreement in the first place;
2. You made a poor choice in selecting the other party as a potential partner.

**The way
it works**

Jerry Wilson's business supplies spare parts for machine tools and most types of general machinery. He sells these items all over the world. Invariably, they are needed urgently and they must be of the right quality. This means that Jerry's company needs reputable and professional distributors, who can support the local market. "I don't like having exclusive distributors in some markets, because, no sooner than they have signed the deal, they go off the boil.

"Distributors have to earn exclusivity and what we call our 'gold service'. This includes access to a wide range of superior service levels, payment on open account, regular visits by engineering and support staff, and a 90-day payment period. Distributors reach this through a process which involves payment by letter of credit certified by a UK clearing bank, agreed stock and sales targets month by month, and an understanding that, if the arrangement does become exclusive, they will have to stop supplying products which compete directly with ours.

"This gradual process means we end up with workable agreements which may ultimately lead to a full exclusive distributorship but which normally end up short of this." This enables Jerry to keep things on hold or to encourage the local distributor by adding a further benefit as an incentive.

CHECKLIST FOR GETTING IT RIGHT

✓ Make your word your bond.
✓ Take and hold on to authority to sign your contracts.
✓ Build in real benefits of success.
✓ Get them involved in setting targets.
✓ Stage the benefits.
✓ Don't threaten unless you can carry out the threat.

9 SWEAT TACTICS AND ULTIMATUMS

55 | MAKING THEM SWEAT A LITTLE

'... they will feel a greater sense of achievement when the agreement is struck.'

Why make them sweat?

The best negotiations are conducted fairly; they reflect a sense of mutual trust and respect, and they result in a win-win conclusion. Participants feel they would enjoy negotiating with each other in the future. Why, then, should you want to make your opponent sweat a little?

In many negotiations, you might not feel the need to make your opponents particularly anxious. However, there is nothing contrary to fair play in stringing them along a little, making them feel, from time to time, that a satisfactory conclusion is in some doubt. At the very least, they are likely to feel a greater sense of achievement when an agreement is finally reached.

When to use the tactic

However, there are situations when this tactic is particularly appropriate. For example, if you feel they are trying to pressurise you with unnecessary deadlines or if you suspect they are playing the 'nice man, nasty man' tactic, you may need to regain the upper hand. Alternatively, you may feel they are being particularly difficult over minor points and you want to re-establish your authority. You want your decisions to be at the fulcrum of the negotiations – not theirs.

There are, of course, a range of tactics you can choose from. These include:

- Playing the reluctant buyer/seller;
- Creating your own higher authority as a stumbling block; and
- Suspending negotiations altogether;
- Withdrawing an offer already proposed; and
- Creating the impression that these difficult tactics have made you lose heart and you see little point in continuing.

Your aims

Your aim is to seize the initiative, and to put pressure on them. You hope they will be distracted from focusing on their key issues, and concentrate instead on keeping the negotiations afloat. Of course, to achieve this favourable condition, you must have something they want and they must not be able to obtain it too easily from another supplier.

The pros and cons

There are several potential advantages in making the opposition sweat a little:

- You can eventually appear helpful in unblocking the problem;
- You can gain influence for future negotiations;
- You may help your opponents to feel very pleased, and perhaps even grateful, for what they eventually achieve.

Of course, they might make life more difficult for you if they understand the tactic you are using. At worst, they may pull out of the negotiations altogether but this is unlikely if you have applied the tactic under the right conditions.

The way it works   J A Bartrams act as sales agents for three engineering firms in the Midlands. They market gauges of varying kinds, but specialise in pressure gauges.

Bartrams have five lease-cars obtained on a three-year, renewable contract from a national car-leasing company. The contract was due for renewal and the leasing company agreed that Bartrams could place their order with a local garage of their choosing. The sale of the five new cars would be attractive to any garage and Jim Gates was determined to achieve certain aims in the purchase.

In particular, he was keen to ensure that courtesy cars would always be available when the lease-cars were in the garage for servicing or repair. The garage said there would be no problem but were obviously reluctant to put the agreement in writing. Jim could understand their reluctance but was not prepared to accept an oral assertion. He and his colleagues could not work without their cars.

Jim first let the garage know that he was very interested in buying and then negotiated on extras, upholstery and finish. The garage was certain that a deal would be struck but would not give way on the courtesy cars. Jim's reaction was to play the reluctant buyer, to inform the garage that he would look elsewhere, and actively to open negotiations with another garage. The original garage relented at this point.

CHECKLIST FOR GETTING IT RIGHT

✓ Use the tactic to break a deadlock.
✓ Ensure you use it under the right conditions.
✓ Let them sweat for long enough but not for too long. Timing is important.
✓ If your opponent relents, be generous where you can.
✓ Finalise the deal as quickly as possible.

'... don't let them gain the upper hand – put yourself in the driving seat ...'

Speed and timing can be everything in a negotiation. If you wait for the other person to make the first move, you are in danger of letting them gain the upper hand. If you get your arguments in first, it can be hard for the person to find a way out of the situation. It's a simple tactic, but very effective.

Of course, it only really works where you are sure of your arguments and your position. It won't be appropriate for the early stages in a negotiation, where each side is testing the water and trying to find out as much as they can about the other.

The way it works

Steve Madison is the production manager of a food manufacturer.

"Pulling the rug out from under them doesn't mean you have to adopt bullying tactics and force your own view of the world on them. All it requires is for you to be assertive and take a lead position in the negotiations. This tactic has worked well for me on several occasions.

"Recently, for example, I used it on one of our canning suppliers, who was trying to wriggle out of paying for some materials of ours they had lost. We often print more labels for our cans than we need. Normally, we ask for our canning supplier to return the surplus to us. Occasionally they forget to do this. Instead they hold on to them for us.

"On this occasion I asked them to send over the spare labels for a particular can I knew they had hung on to, as we wanted to use a different company for the processing. I didn't get a response at first and, when I chased them, our contact tried to make out they had sent all of them back to us. Although they normally do this for us I was 100 per cent certain they had hung on to these particular labels. I didn't want to have to pay for them to be reprinted. The difficulty was how to prove they were in the wrong. Their representative said their delivery notes proved they had been returned to us, so I asked him to fax a copy over to me.

"I didn't believe him for a moment. But I was concerned they might pull a fast one on me and produce a forged delivery note. I gathered all the paperwork together with the delivery sheets. If labels were being returned to us they would mark their delivery notes with the number of surplus copies that were enclosed with the cans. If they retained any labels the delivery note said nothing. The delivery note for the labels in question made no mention of any surplus labels being returned to us. I put all the evidence together and immediately faxed it over to him before he could get anything to me.

"He knew it would be pointless to argue the case further and we had a credit note for the lost labels by return. By getting in there first I had successfully pulled the rug out from under them and won the negotiation."

Watch out how you use it
You need to be a bit careful with this tactic as, if it's used inappropriately, it could back-fire on you. For example, instead of being seen to take control of a situation, your assertiveness may be interpreted as forcing the other party into a direction in which they don't want to go. Watch out that you don't put words into their mouths, or come across as an overbearing boor. You may achieve a result in the short term but, when it comes to getting a longer-term commitment, they will probably refuse you. Remember, people like to do business with people like themselves. If you come across as a presumptuous bully they will decide they are better off not doing business with you in future.

CHECKLIST FOR GETTING IT RIGHT

✓ Don't wait for the other person to make the first move.
✓ Get your arguments in first – take the lead.
✓ Use this in the later stages of a negotiation, not as your opening shot.
✓ Be assertive, but don't bully.
✓ Remember that people like to do business with people like themselves.

'Nothing takes the wind out of the bully's sails like well documented evidence.'

Every single problem or challenge that arise in any negotiation can usually be countered by proper planning and preparation. In the case of the bully or arrogant know-it-all, it is only when we know, for a fact, that we are likely to encounter them, that planning can help. Unfortunately, the most pleasant of people, those with whom we have had many negotiations and conversations can, for some strange reason, turn into bullies. Their normal calmness is suddenly replace by outbursts of anger and shouting.

Watch out for the 'control freak'

This usually happens when a 'control freak' doesn't get their own way. There are a number of ways to deal with the problem.

1. Proper planning. Proper planning plays its part in every negotiation. I like to think of it in this way. I imagine that the negotiation I am about to enter into is the last commercial conversation and meeting I will ever have in my life and that the whole of my future financial security rests in the outcome of the meeting. Then planning doesn't seem such a chore, doesn't seem a waste of time, doesn't seem unimportant. I can recall one particular meeting which was almost that important to my future financial well-being and proper planning saw me through.

2. Proper preparation. When entering a negotiation, any negotiation, let alone one where you may have tackle the know-it-all, it is essential to prepare the documentation and proof of facts you will need or that the other party may present. Nothing takes the wind out of the bully's sails like well documented evidence. Edward de Bono in his superb book *Six Thinking Hats* suggests that, at a meeting we should don different hats to force us to think in different ways. The "White Hat" thinking must be supported by facts that can be proved. This hat, for many, is the most difficult to wear. People make assumptions, jump to conclusions and generally use 'gut feelings' to make decisions. Gut feelings are good; however, assumptions and false conclusions have ruined many a promising outcome. Be well prepared.

3. Ask for proof. If the other party is arrogant and demonstrating know-it-all characteristics, it will be common for them to use argument to support their case. Ask for proof! Usually they will ignore the request and continue with their tirade or assumptions; let them! Then ask for proof again. Keep asking for proof until they back down or provide it. Usually, they can't.

4. Take breaks. To calm a situation, if the know-it-all has become too aggressive, take a break. This break may also give you the opportunity to investigate the assumptions you have been given. Let the other side know that you need the break to undertake investigations into their statements. If their statements are spurious, they will back down.

5. Change the venue. A change of venue often sees a change in attitude in all of the parties to a negotiation. Suggest a change when the atmosphere has become too charged with emotion to allow sensible movement forward. The break alone can help the process. The new venue should be selected with care. Change the know-it-all's position from head of the table to the side of the table. Or if they have been at the side of the table, place them at the end, as a recognition of their power, so that their words now do not need to make the point of their superiority.

Let them blow off steam

6. Remain calm! Perhaps the easiest way to tackle the know-it-all, particularly the arrogant kind, is to remain calm. Let them blow off steam, let them get angry, let them state and restate their points again and again and again. Just stay calm, secure in the knowledge that you can outlast them.

7. Use the repeat method. This is an extremely useful method to bring someone back to the point. Often the arrogance comes to the surface when the know-it-all doesn't know it all and uses bullying tactics to cover up that fact. Simply repeating your position or statement again and again works wonders.

Attending one extremely sensitive meeting some years ago, I was met by an army of people on the other side of the negotiation. Two lawyers, two accountants, five directors, the company secretary and two stockbrokers. The discussion was regarding the payment of the second tranche of the money on a company-sale earn-out arrangement. The chairman of the board responded to my initial question with a 10-minute outburst ... letting him finish, I simply asked the same question again and continued asking it until I had the answer I required. Sometimes, calmness and patience are the best weapons.

8. I have to refer it! You will be able to resist any 'steamroller' tactics by stating that you have to refer the matter to someone or something else:

- Your immediate superior
- Your subordinates
- Team members
- The contract
- Accountants
- Solicitors
- The stock exchange
- Your parent company
- The board of directors

9. Don't take it personally. The know-it-all probably uses this tactic in all negotiations. Usually, we haven't been singled out to receive the treatment.

125

Avoid taking it personally; treat it as an amusing part of the negotiation process.

10. Treat them in the same way. By this I do *not* mean that we should act in the way they act ! Far from it. Simply continue to treat the other party exactly how you would wish to be treated. If you remain calm and polite, despite their boorish behaviour, they will eventually calm down and treat you with that same respect.

CHECKLIST FOR GETTING IT RIGHT

✓ Undertake planning of every aspect.
✓ Prepare proof and documentation.
✓ Take breaks.
✓ Remain calm.
✓ Use 'we' language rather than 'I' language.

WHEN VEILED THREATS ARE MADE

'You must do what you must do, but it doesn't change our view.'

Making threats, however veiled, is all about perceived power. Power can be real or imaginary but you only really find out when you are forced into implementing the sanction or threat. If you threaten the other party, the threat is only as powerful as your willingness to implement it. The veiled threat is made when the other party, while still wishing to continue the negotiation with you, hints at all manner of difficulties that you may experience if you do not reach agreement with them.

Note it but ignore it

You should only take a veiled threat seriously if you know that you are in a weak position and you know that they know. You should ask yourself "Why are they so anxious to get me to agree to this?". "What have I missed?" Asking these questions challenges you to reassess your situation and theirs, and the balance of power. Most business negotiations take place in an ever-changing environment. Timing can be crucial to the outcome of the negotiation, for one party or another. Slight changes in share price, raw material availability, competitor activity, exchange rates, seasonality, and government interference, can all shift the balance of power away from or towards either party. An exposed weakness can either lead to a veiled threat from the other party, hoping to gain an advantage, or a veiled threat from the weaker party, trying to hide it.

Expose it

Expose it by asking for clarification. You are told by the company that you are negotiating with that there might be a need to look for parts of the contract to be undertaken by other suppliers. You challenge by asking: "Are you saying that you are having discussions with other suppliers concerning all or part of this contract?". This will shift the balance of power. You will either get a denial from the company or they will find it hard to hide the fact that they are also negotiating with others.

Show them it doesn't bother you. Hard to do if it does but a very powerful way of countering a threat is to show that you are not bothered whether the other party carries out their threat or not. "You must do what you must do but it doesn't change our view that ..." counters any threat made by the other party. Having made the veiled threat and seen that you have brushed it aside immediately, the other party is then in a weaker position.

Try not to be too dependent

Veiled threats are often made when one party has the upper hand and wants the other party to concede a point. The party in the stronger position does not need to threaten openly but, simply by implying what could happen, they get their way. Small companies dependent on one or two key accounts, sub-contractors in very competitive industries such as the building industry, companies that have invested heavily in new plant and machinery in order to meet orders from a new customer, are all examples of companies that have put themselves into a position where the veiled threat is likely to work.

If your company is dependent on one or two key accounts, try to build in some dependency the other way. Create a linkage with the end-user, if you are part of chain. Develop specialist services which set you apart from other companies. Get to know and understand your customer's business so well that you would be hard to replace in the short term. In this way, you reduce the chance of your customer gaining from a veiled threat by drawing their attention to their need for your products or services.

The way it works

Holland has a well earned reputation for being a country where negotiations have become an art form. Because Holland is so dependent on trade for the health of its economy, the Dutch have become very good negotiators.

Richard Hunter's company had been supplying their products to Holland for several years but only to one customer. The customer was a very large Dutch co-operative, with one of the largest processing plants in Europe. "The Dutch knew we wanted more business from them and also knew that they were our only customers" said Richard. "They always drove a very hard bargain and invariably dropped the name of one or two of our competitors into the conversation. For two years our business with the co-operative grew but with very small profit margins. The co-operative was making good profits out of the business they were doing with us."

Richard did two things to try to alter the balance of power.

1. He persuaded his Dutch customer to arrange visits to their customers who were using the products that Richard supplied. These end-users confirmed how successful Richard's products were in comparison to products from other suppliers.
2. He made contact with several much smaller potential customers in other parts of Holland and managed to do some much more profitable business with these new contacts. He then managed to get a press release into the Dutch trade journals, emphasising the potential of this new business for both his company and his new Dutch customers.

"The result was that we continued to be dependent on the co-operative but I knew that we were not as weak as they would have me believe. I managed to reduce the significance of their veiled threat."

CHECKLIST FOR GETTING IT RIGHT

✓ Veiled threats have implications for both parties.
✓ If you can, note it but then ignore it.
✓ Expose it for what it is.
✓ Work out ways of redressing the balance.

59 | WHAT TO DO WHEN THEY SAY "TAKE IT OR LEAVE IT"

'An ultimatum should only be used as a last resort.'

The ultimatum can be a good ploy. It closes down the other side's options for side-stepping the issues (your issues). But it must be used very sparingly and only at the right time or it can weaken your position. What it says is that there is no further negotiation available – period.

Don't close your options off too early

If that is the case, you have also closed down your options. Therefore, you had better be extremely certain that the position you have established is the only one you will countenance. And how are you to know? What if they were about to introduce a whacking great concession? Many have missed out on good opportunities by playing that card too soon.

So that is the essential weakness of the ploy; that weakness (the soft underbelly, if you like) is where we aim when we want to counter it.

- "That's the price. Take it or leave it."
  "For how many?"
  "Er... how many did you want?"
  "I haven't decided yet."

or ...

- "That's all we'll pay. Take it or leave it."
  "Great! I'll take it! Goodbye."
  "Er ... just a minute."

It is a last resort. If either of you try to play this card too early, in order to be seen to be flexing your muscles, you will be wide open to being knocked down.

The way it works

Even if the time seems to be right, the circumstances could be wrong. Tactic 100 discusses the importance of getting inside the other person's head. If you issue an ultimatum without looking at it from the perspective of the opposition, you could make a serious mistake.

Joshua Ravenscroft, paper dealer, had one such experience. "It looked a fairly straightforward deal, and I had brought with me the lad who would be looking after the account. The guy on the other side was bright enough, but young – a bit wet behind the ears, if you know what I mean. He started pushing me on the price, and then came out with it – take it or leave it! I took a deep breath, and then asked if there was somewhere my lad could wait while we spoke privately.

"When we were alone, I spoke to this geezer like a Dutch Uncle. I told him never – never – to issue an ultimatum to someone who had a junior present. That lad would be coming to me for a pay-rise sometime and if he felt that I could be done-over by an ultimatum, he'd be trying it on all the time. So, although I was quite happy with the price he was asking me to take, I was going to have to leave it. I knew he'd hate that, because we were already well below the price he was paying elsewhere – I do my homework.

Don't try to kid a kidder

"He started backtracking nineteen to the dozen! Asked me whether there was a way out. I said the only way out was to call the lad back and explain that I had, 'made you see the light'. But that meant a higher price!

"I assured him that, as soon as I reasonably could, I would give him a 'loyalty discount' which would put his price right but in the meantime he'd be paying over the odds – take it or leave it! He took it."

CHECKLIST FOR GETTING IT RIGHT

✓ Use an ultimatum only as a last resort.
✓ If someone gives you one, immediately make them think they were too early with it.
✓ Get inside their head and look at your ultimatum from their perspective, before you issue it.
✓ Don't try to kid a kidder!

'... but what on earth will my boss say about that?'

People often hide their fears. In everyday life, we may be wary of telling the whole world we are claustrophobic, or frightened of spiders or the dark. In business, too, we all have our fears; one on a par with the above is being frightened of people who say "I am from Head Office – and here to help you"! ... but we digress. In negotiating, people have fears too, and they are unlikely to volunteer them to those with whom they negotiate.

Types of fear The first step to using other people's fear to bring power to your negotiation is to have the range of possibilities in mind. These are too broad to categorise comprehensively here, but the following are examples of some of the main ones:

- **Emotional**: "I just don't like to lose". This attitude can lead to heels being dug in for no clear logical reason and can apply to fear of the overall process going wrong, or when someone has set their heart on getting something agreed 'their way'.

- **Personal**: "If it's agreed that way, it will be best for *me*". This is where the person is fearful that things will not be right for them personally (rather than for their organisation or department, say) unless the agreement goes a certain way.

- **Objective**: "Whatever happens, I simply must get agreement to ...". Here, the fear is of key elements of the deal not turning out right; because this is linked most obviously to the topic of the negotiation, it may be easiest to recognise.

- **Losing face**: "I won't be made to look silly (or incompetent, inexpert or whatever)". This fear can be very powerful and apply to losing face with you, or with others involved, during or after the negotiation.

- **Other people**: "What on earth will my boss say, if I can't even agree .....". Here, the priorities are set not solely by the negotiator, but by others (whose influence may or may not be apparent), in the background.

- **Their competencies being inadequate**: "It is 5 per cent I'm sure, no, I'm not ... think ... think!" This may refer, as for the example stated here, to powers of numeracy or to many other factors. The fear is of getting something wrong, and thus influencing the outcome, but may also link to losing face. Key weaknesses, such as an awareness that they are not as quick on their feet as they would like over, say, figures, can provide particular opportunities.

Identifying opportunities Action here takes two forms:

1 Asking questions: this is, anyway, an inherent part of the negotiation process, but the objective in focus here is to identify priorities, other

131

people being involved, hidden agendas, key issues, etc., in a way that highlights potential fears. It is, after all, not easy to say simply "What's your worst nightmare about this?" (though you might think of exceptions); more often, you have to read between the lines somewhat.

2 Observation: watch the body language – what makes them hesitate, stumble or otherwise show indications of worry? Care is necessary here. Body language is not an exact science and people will attempt to hide fears, so avoid letting the prospect of an opportunity that would help you lead to hasty assumptions.

The way it works
Again there are two main ways forward as to how the knowledge gained can be used:

1 Stealth: you simply bear in mind the element you have identified (perhaps with a little judicious testing along the way); you don't declare it but you use it to unsettle their progress, perhaps refusing to discuss a point, yet belittling it "Well, I don't suppose either of us have much concern about that, let's take ... first, that's much more important" or otherwise casting doubt on it being dealt with in a straightforward way.

2 Confrontation: you attack the area feared, perhaps making it very clear that this bit is going to be a battle "Now, let's see about ... I shall have to drive a hard bargain here" or: "I'm sure this a priority for you, but it is for me too." You can even compound the effect, by judicious mentions at various stages of the conversation. Actively conjure up an image of a small, dark cupboard full of large spiders and one more element of the total process can be organised to increase your power.

CHECKLIST FOR GETTING IT RIGHT

✓ Be aware of the range of possible fears.
✓ Discover specific fears: questions and observation.
✓ Decide how openly to use the knowledge gained.
✓ Play on the fear, appropriately to what you hope to gain.

10 WHEN YOUR BACK IS TO THE WALL

61 | WHAT TO DO WHEN THEY SAY SOMETHING IS A NON-NEGOTIABLE ITEM

'A non-negotiable item can be negotiable when the facts are presented.'

The non-negotiable item

In reality, there are not usually many non-negotiable items in business. All items or negotiating issues have a value and that value is relative. Find something of higher value and the non-negotiable item is suddenly negotiable. Typical 'non-negotiable' items are:

- bottom price,
- delivery time and
- quality specifications.

Avoid argument

The best policy, when faced with a non-negotiable item, is not to argue about it but simply to recognise it. You could try to 'flinch', as though you have just been stabbed, to let your opponent know that you find this troubling. However, arguing is usually a fairly negative process.

Prise it open

You could, at this point, try probing the item, looking for small cracks to prise it open. Or you could test it for validity. For example, an estate agent might have been told by a potential house-buyer "My absolute maximum is £120,000. I really cannot negotiate beyond that". The estate agent's reply might be, "So if I find a really magnificent property at £125,000, one you would give your eye teeth for, shall I just show it to other clients?".

Set it aside

Another ploy is to use the set-aside technique. With this, you simply acknowledge the stipulation and then move on to other points. Here, you are attempting to achieve agreement on a number of items, to give the talks a sense of momentum and achievement. When you return to the 'non-negotiable' item, your opponent will be much more reluctant to throw away the progress already made.

Life could be so much better

If the non-negotiable item is important to you, here is a final way of dealing with it. After applying the set-aside technique, develop a picture gradually, showing how much easier the talks would be without this stipulation. You open up avenues that could be explored but for the stumbling block.

Get a return

Of course, the item might actually be of little or no value to you. Nevertheless, you should not throw it away lightly. Indeed, your aim should be to exact in return a high penalty, a concession that is of high value to you. You can appear to be fully justified in doing so, because your opponent has made life so difficult.

Is it really non-negotiable?

When your opponents say an item is non-negotiable, they do so for one of three reasons:

134

- It really is non-negotiable.
- They are using a ploy.
- They think the item is non-negotiable when in fact it is not. They may be able to go back to higher authority and find more flexibility.

If the item really is non-negotiable, you may cause irritation if you push too hard. If it is a ploy you are pushing against, they may give way and seek something from you.

Organising a conference

Brenda Marston is a senior partner in Congress Ltd, a consultancy specialising in conference organisation. She was negotiating with a large grocery chain, who had approached her about organising a national conference for senior managers from all branches. Their non-negotiable item was the schedule. The conference had to be held in five months' time.

The item was obviously of considerable interest to Brenda and she was very concerned about the implications and genuinely felt that she could do a much better job for the firm with more time. At the same time, she did not want to lose the contract.

She showed surprise at the schedule, acknowledged it and moved on to other areas, reaching agreement on such matters as her fees, regional location and general conference facilities. However, she carefully came back to the schedule on a number of occasions, showing the losses incurred by an early date. One or two of the best speakers would not be available; the best conference hall was booked; the time of year was not best suited.

Eventually, when her opponent saw the advantages of a later date, he went back to higher authority. The non-negotiable item became negotiable when the facts were presented.

 ## CHECKLIST FOR GETTING IT RIGHT

✓ Perhaps flinch, but do not immediately argue.
✓ Probe and test for validity.
✓ Or set it aside and agree other items first.
✓ Place your own value on the item.
✓ Aim for something in return, if you accept.
✓ Beware the false non-negotiable item raised as a ploy.

IT'S BETTER TO LOSE THE BATTLE BUT WIN THE WAR

'Striving to win everything can lead to a stalemate.'

The analogy with warfare

In one sense, an analogy with warfare is misleading, since in war, a win-lose outcome is what each commander seeks. Montgomery believed in ensuring a high probability of success before engaging in battle and certainly did not look forward to the next war. In negotiation, a win-win is usually the best outcome and opponents in a satisfactory set of talks look forward to future engagements.

However, in a narrower sense, the title of this item is true. Negotiations are seldom about one issue and each side usually has a set of objectives which are of varying values to them. It is unrealistic of one side to expect to win all its points and the other side to lose all theirs – unless of course there is absolutely no chance of further negotiation. But who can tell what the future holds?

The purpose of negotiation

The purpose of negotiation is to gain one's major objectives but, at the same time, to be aware of the opposition's objectives, and, if possible, to ensure a win-win conclusion. Striving to win everything can easily lead to a lose-lose situation or a stalemate.

Gain concessions in return

None of this is to suggest that you should throw away negotiating points too easily. You should aim to get something in return for a point conceded but you should always try to keep a proper perspective throughout the proceedings. Be clear about the important issues and be prepared to give way on a minor point, if it contributes towards the achievement of an important one.

Give and take

Essentially this point is about the need to give and take, provided you end up taking more than you give in terms of your own values. Ideally, because you and your opponent value differently the negotiating issues, you could each conclude by giving away on lesser points and achieving your major objectives. Thus the conclusion favours both sides and you can continue to experience an amicable relationship with your opponent.

Union negotiations

Michael Tanner is the chief personnel officer in a local-government district council. Since this particular authority is not party to the national pay agreement, it has to do its own negotiating with the trades unions.

The aim, each year, is to reach agreement before 1 April, so that increases can be awarded from that date. Thus, in February, negotiations were taking place in preparation for the new financial year. On one side were three elected members, advised by Michael Tanner; on the other were three union representatives.

The employers' main objective was to agree a wage settlement in the range 2.5–3 per cent, the percentage increase to be applied equally to all grades. On their part, the union sought an unspecified flat-rate increase with employer commitment to:

- introduce job evaluation for all posts;
- a training-needs analysis and
- extra time off for trades union officials.

Clearly, there were additional costs implicit in each of these activities and the employers did not wish to introduce any of them. They were not opposed to them in principle but their need to set a budget and their fear of being capped made them feel very vulnerable if they agreed to any additional expenditure.

They lost a battle but not the war
The elected members wished to fight all the union proposals but Michael Tanner was able to persuade them that, to avoid deadlock, they must be prepared to lose one battle. In the event, they gave way on the training-needs analysis and on giving extra time off for trades union officials. They settled on a wage increase of 3 per cent, applicable to all grades, but did not give way on job evaluation. They had lost a battle, but not the war.

CHECKLIST FOR GETTING IT RIGHT

✓ Generally seek a win-win conclusion.
✓ Do not aim to win everything.
✓ Gain something in return for each concession.
✓ Try to ensure that each concession is of relatively low value to you.
✓ When you do concede a point, make your opponent feel that you have given up something of real value to you.

63 | SAVING YOUR FACE WHEN YOU FALL ON YOUR NOSE

'Quietly and firmly apologise.'

Everyone makes mistakes in negotiations, even the most seasoned negotiator. When those mistakes are known only to you (you underestimated the cost of a particular concession, for example), you can put them down to experience and it doesn't take long to recover from them.

People are more forgiving than you think

But when the mistake is very public and everyone knows and notices, it becomes the stuff that nightmares are made of. There is little point in wheeling out the usual platitudes – it is never as bad as it seems, people are more forgiving than you think, they are probably more embarrassed than you are, etc. When it happens to you, it feels dreadful.

The easiest sort of mistake to deal with is where you are arguing a case based on wrong information.

The way it works

Michael Block was new to selling insert space in magazines. His experience to date had been in selling advertising space on the pages of the magazine. He knew he had a very hot prospect in Meridian Audio, because they had been successfully advertising in similar magazines for some time. He pitched the insert rate at £100 per thousand. He knew that Meridian's product sold for £250 and he was quite certain that they would see this as a good deal. Meridian seemed unimpressed and told him that when he could come back at £50 per thousand, they would look at it. Michael assumed that this was simply a price-cutting ploy by Meridian and came back strongly with a slightly improved offer of £95 per thousand. Meridian became irritated and told him again that they would start talking at £50 per thousand. This carried on for a couple of days in the course of ten phone calls. Finally, someone at Meridian told Michael to go away and not come back as he obviously had no idea what their costs were. It transpired that the manufacturing cost of each item was £100 and the cost of printing the inserts added £65 per thousand to the deal. Meridian's suggestion of £50 was based on what profit they could reasonably expect to make on the sale of each product.

Michael had a problem. He had a potential client who thought he was an idiot. He had claimed that the magazine could not afford to drop the insert price below £90 per thousand. He needed to retrieve the situation fast.

The solution is straightforward:

1. Apologise for the mistake. Assure them that it was based on a genuine misunderstanding of the facts and thank them for taking the trouble to explain the situation clearly.
2. Make a new offer based on this information.
3. Find a face-saving formula.

138

Michael came back with an offer of £55 per thousand if Meridian accepted an open insert date. The justification was that Meridian's insert would take the place of one which pulled out at the last minute but which had already been paid for on a non-refundable basis.

But what if the mistake is a social gaffe?

You have just bad-mouthed the local football team. You use the phrase "Jesus Christ!" as an exclamation of surprise and your opposite number quietly says "Please don't blaspheme in this office, it offends many of us".

You express disbelief that anyone would pay good money for model 33X only to be told "We took delivery of 100 units only yesterday".

These mistakes happen when you have misjudged the other side. You will rarely know them well enough safely to tell jokes, or to have an opinion on sport, religion, politics or social issues. Yet the pressure is there for you to try to align yourself closely with their values, because the more like them you appear to be, the easier the negotiation will be. So train yourself early on to listen before you speak and resist the temptation to come out with an original comment in any of these areas.

But it's too late – you have already said the unsayable. What do you do?

Never ignore it and hope that it will go away. It will not go away in your mind and you will be distracted, wondering who noticed and how offended they were.

Quietly and firmly apologise. "I am sorry. It was a thoughtless remark and not one I particularly mean, either" or "I am sorry. I didn't mean to say that. I don't even believe it" or "I'm sorry. That came out all wrong and was not what I meant to say at all!".

Then look around the table with a rueful smile, pick up your papers and say "May we return to the business in hand. Can you tell me how many units a week you would be interested in taking?".

CHECKLIST FOR GETTING IT RIGHT

✓ Don't be drawn into discussions of sensitive topics.
✓ Keep your own views to yourself.
✓ Always apologise immediately and without fuss.
✓ Return the discussion to the subject of the negotiation – a question is a good way of doing this.

64

WHAT TO DO WHEN THEY BRING IN THE EXPERTS

'One who is skilled in any art or science: a specialist: a scientific or professional witness ...' (Chambers Twentieth Century Dictionary)

An expert witness is used to support one side's arguments or rebut the other side's counter-proposals. In negotiations, experts are used to reduce the value of your proposals, make you feel inferior and generally to give the impression that the other party's proposal is very much better than your own. Using experts is all about shifting the balance of power away from you. There are a number of counter-measures that you can take to stop this happening.

Ask who's coming

Always ask who will be present at any negotiation and what their rôle is in the negotiation. They may still surprise you but, if they do bring along an expert without telling you, you can simply side-step any question from the expert by saying that, because they did not tell you that Professor X was coming to the meeting, you would prefer the Professor to make a list of any technical points, which you will then ask your own experts to answer at a later date. They failed to tell you and you should labour this point confidently, without being defensive.

Flattery can work wonders

Flattery gets you a long way, if the expert is unknown to you. Shake their hand, tell them it's a pleasure to meet them, and suggest you will try and do your best to answer to their technical questions. This is particularly useful if negotiating overseas, where, unless the expert is world-renowned, you are unlikely ever to have heard of them. Keep all discussions to technical areas you are experienced in. The expert will try to reduce your own power, by referring to obscure reports, name-dropping, and bringing in their own research. Test how expert they really are with a few well prepared questions, to which you know the answers, but never allow this to develop into a 'head to head' contest. Ask for copies of their technical reports, so that you can study them and learn more about their area of expertise.

Sideline the expert ... politely

Sideline the expert by immediately explaining that you are responsible for the commercial operations of the business and what you wish to discuss and negotiate are the commercial arrangements both sides are keen to enter into. Every time they ask you technical questions, make a note of them, answer those which you can with confidence, and refer the others to your own experts after the discussions have finished.

Have your own experts. Let the experts fight it out while you get on with the real negotiations. If the other party bring along their expert in water-treatment systems, you bring yours. If they have a financial guru with them, have yours. Every time their expert gets involved, ask yours to respond and then follow with a searching question of your own. If this goes on for a while, you and your opposite number will soon find a way of stopping it and getting down to the real negotiation. A useful suggestion is to propose that your experts and theirs get together separately in another room, while you get on with the main parts of the proposals.

Experts are there to influence the outcome but you are the person who decides that outcome.

If the negotiation is about a very technical subject, try to understand the key principles and how they may affect what you are trying to achieve. Don't become the expert, as this may well get in the way of your negotiating skills, but keep focused on the result you wish to achieve.

Third-parties can be useful
Use third-parties to reduce any inference by their expert that your proposals are technically inferior. For example, you may be supplying your product or service to a major organisation known for its very high specification requirements. By referring to this existing arrangement you imply, without actually saying so, that if you are able to meet company X's specifications, you don't feel that you will have difficulty in meeting company Y's.

The way it works
Michael Chisholm sells veterinary equipment to universities, hospitals, and private customers. He is not a vet but is experienced in dealing with experts. "I negotiate business with the purchasing manager and find that I am often confronted with either a vet or a professor of animal science. They ask technical and complex questions, designed to show how much they know and how little I understand. The purchasing manager usually takes no part, other than to observe. I use a combination of flattery, third-party references and agreeing to refer questions to my own technical team at head office. After a while, the purchasing manager has heard enough and wants to negotiate the business I have come to discuss. The expert usually has more 'pressing' matters to attend to."

 ## CHECKLIST FOR GETTING IT RIGHT

✓ Find out who is coming.
✓ Match expert with expert.
✓ Experts may try to influence the outcome but you are the negotiator. Do not negotiate with them.
✓ Remember why they are there.
✓ Don't alienate them but do sideline them.

65

WHAT TO DO WHEN THEY ARE BEING 'ECONOMICAL WITH THE TRUTH'

'You've heard the story, but is it the whole story ?'

Of all the skills of communication, perhaps one of the most important is our ability to spot when someone is being 'economical with the truth'. There are a number of key gestures we can identify and a number of ways of dealing with the situations. As with the reading of all body-language signals, care must be taken. A nose rub may be just that, a nose rub to deal with an itch or irritation; however it may be an indication of nervousness or lying.

1. Hand over mouth I
If someone puts their hand over their mouth when they are talking, this may indicate that they are trying to stop the words coming out. We have seen young children covering their faces when they tell a lie. "No, I didn't break it!" When someone feels nervous about the information they are giving, they often exhibit hand-to-face gestures, particularly hand or finger touching the lips.

2. Hand over mouth II
When a listener puts their hand over their mouth they may be indicating that they are concerned with the information they are receiving or that they disagree or that they think the speaker is lying. If this gesture is accompanied by "I agree with you!" that statement may well be far from the truth. When talking, it is advisable to watch the hand movements in particular of the other person, the listener. Those movements may well show their true feelings about what you have said.

3. Eye pull and ear pull
Pulling the corner of the eye or pulling the ear lobe shows that the person exhibiting this gesture, whilst talking, may be being economical with the truth. It said that actors were taught to pull at the corner of their eyes when telling lies. This gesture would be read by the audience as proof of that lie and give greater credibility to the actor's performance.

4. Flattening tones
Often, when someone lies, the tones of their voice, previously animated, become flatter. Their voice takes on a calmness which is mismatched with the content of their speech. Active listening easily reveals these changes.

5. Restricted movement
Hands that flew about adding movement to the words . . . suddenly cease. Pacing becomes ... standing still. The head suddenly stops its movement. Why? Well this sudden restriction in movement can be a strong indication that the person is trying to be ... more in control. It is this very act of control that indicates a lack of control or in other words ... a lie!

6. Listen to the content
"Oh what a tangled web we weave, when first we practise to deceive!" It's true, isn't it, that, if we attempt to be 'economical with the truth', we need to have, not only an excellent memory, but excellent recall as well? So often, the liar will trip themselves up with inconsistencies. Their stories

simply do not stack up. One piece of information contradicts another. If you have a concern that the other party is spinning stories, a well planned and prepared series of questions will be a way to catch them out. This is based on the following simple example.

Question 1: "What is 5 + 4?". Answer: "9".

Later ... Question 2: "What is 9 – 5?". The answer should be 4.

If you are able to design a series of questions which cross-check each other, then continuity or lack of it can easily be recognised.

7. Listen actively
The key skill in business and negotiations is that of active listening. Using this skill alone will uncover most situations where someone is being economical with the truth.

8. Take notes
Having an agenda and a series of pre-planned questions on a questionnaire form will create a format for good note-taking. Where you have a concern about information received, reference to previous notes may well indicate the area of discrepancy. So often in negotiations, good-quality notes aren't taken and errors are made. In the 'heat of battle' it is nevertheless essential that time is taken to make accurate records. A tape recorder, with the other person's permission, may be one solution. I have even known people use a hidden tape recorder, when the negotiation and its outcome warranted such apparently underhand action. Having two people involved can also help: one to talk and one to write.

9. Use review breaks
Take regular breaks, to review the information you have received and look for errors or untruthful statements. This is where having two people per side really pays dividends.

10. Ask for proof
If statements are being made which are obviously untrue, ask for proof and refuse to continue the negotiation until proof has been provided. Continuing with the two parties concerned working from different assumptions is a guaranteed recipe for failure. If necessary, reschedule the negotiation for a time when proof can be provided.

Whenever you realise than someone has been economical with the truth, that perhaps you have caught them lying ... let them off the hook. Let them retract the statement and save face. Saying such things as "I think I probably misunderstood what you said, did you mean ...?" may be a better resolution than "You misled me!". "Perhaps I didn't take my notes properly, could you just restate you thoughts about ...?" would also work well. Let them off the hook, if a successful outcome is what you seek from the negotiation.

CHECKLIST FOR GETTING IT RIGHT

✓ Take good notes.
✓ Listen actively.
✓ Ask a series of pre-planned questions.
✓ Have two people at the meeting.
✓ Let them save face.

66

USING HUMOUR TO 'DEFUSE' A TENSE SITUATION

'... use it to lower the temperature in a tense situation.'

Most people welcome humour

Nearly all people enjoy humour at work and most would agree that life would be extremely dull without it. Humour helps to oil the wheels in on-going relationships and to prevent friction. It can also help to lower the temperature in a particularly tense situation.

Forms of humour

Some people have a natural touch, a facility for seeing the funny side of everything, to find the odd perspective which the rest of us have missed. Some derive humour by juxtaposing two incompatible events. Others are funny simply because of the figures of speech they use when telling a story and some people use facial expressions to make us laugh.

I well remember a Welshman, almost inevitably called Dai, who could recount mildly amusing events and make them seem hysterically amusing. Of course, he had an excellent grasp of the language and could look funny but it was his infectious sense of life that really touched people.

Problems with humour

Of course, humour can also present us with problems and we need to exercise care in using it in negotiations. One problem is that we do not all share the same sense of humour. Another is that much humour is directed at someone else's misfortune.

Sometimes we can get away with a form of humour, if we know our audience, that we would not use in general company. Humour is very much a matter of personal taste and requires sensitivity in its use. If unsure, we are best sticking to obviously inoffensive comments or else humour directed against ourselves. Self-deprecating stories usually go down quite well and nobody suffers in the process.

Favour light asides

Nor does the humour have to cause outright laughter. Light asides, such as the following, help to alleviate the rather tense atmosphere:

- "If I stay here any later, colleagues, I'm going to have some really tough negotiating to do when I get home to my partner."
- "You people are really hard. I have to keep looking to see if I've still got my shirt on."

In this last example, it is highly unlikely that your opponent would be offended. More likely he or she will be amused and probably even a little flattered.

Be careful with this one

Perhaps one of the most apt stories, bearing in mind the overall subject of this publication, is one concerning George Bernard Shaw. However it is not a story one could use against one's opponent and hope to reach a satisfactory conclusion to the talks.

Shaw was said to have been dining with a woman when he asked her if, assuming he were to offer her one million pounds, she would go to bed with him. She paused only for a moment to reflect that one million pounds was a great deal of money before agreeing that she would find it difficult to resist.

"Well would you do it for ten shillings?" was his next approach. "Certainly not!" she replied, somewhat sharply, "What do you take me for?". "I thought we'd already established that," said Shaw "Now we're negotiating about the price."

Relationships and communication

Humour, then, can be useful when it relaxes the tension in the negotiating situation and, of course, there is a close tie between relationships and communication. The better the communication, the better the relationship is likely to be; the better the relationship, the better the communication is likely to be – and so on:

The potential disadvantages are that humour can backfire and cause offence.

CHECKLIST FOR GETTING IT RIGHT

✓ Assess the company carefully before using humour.
✓ Fit the humour to the company of people you are with.
✓ Avoid sexist and racist comments, and extreme forms of vulgarity.
✓ If in doubt, use gentler, lighter forms of humour.
✓ Wit is usually appreciated.
✓ Self-deprecating humour will not cause offence.

67 | WHAT TO DO WHEN THEY KEEP HARPING ON THE SAME OLD TUNE

'Take their record, break it across your knee and find another tune that you can both sing along to.'

Negotiating with a stubborn individual, who refuses to move from a point, can be really hard work. Just when you think you've made real progress and moved the debate onwards and upwards, they 'reset themselves to zero' and take the negotiation back to square one. How can you reset their expectations and fix this recurring blockage?

Have you sold the solution correctly?
For the salesperson, if you encounter a situation such as this, ask yourself, 'Have I adequately uncovered their needs and proposed a solution that will fix the pain they are feeling?' There has got to be a reason why they keep returning to this fundamental objection and you need to address it. Let's work through an example.

Your customer is going to buy a new computer system. They like what you offer and your system matches their overall specifications. You meet the finance director, to negotiate the shape of the final deal. Between you, you quickly reach a price that is fair and move on to negotiating other details, such as delivery, training and installation dates. However, out of the blue, the finance director says:

"I don't understand why this system is going to cost so much: I thought technology was meant to be coming down in price?" and a little later, "my first system never cost me this much!".

You ignore the first and second comments and hope that the finance director doesn't want to reopen the debate on price. Unfortunately, it isn't going to be that easy and, within five minutes, he makes another comment about the cost of the system. What do you do? How do you tackle his concerns and get the negotiation back on track?

Is he genuinely concerned about price?
Firstly, you need to assess whether the technique is being used deliberately, or whether your opponent is genuinely concerned about the price. Secondly, you need to ask yourself, what is the real question I am being asked? Is it that:

- Your system is too expensive and why can't we have a big discount?
- Will the benefits we receive outweigh the cost of the investment we will have to make?

Don't be alarmed if you decide that the finance director is following a negotiation technique based on a single-position negotiating stance. This technique will make it very difficult for you to tackle other areas of the negotiation and will, if unchecked, keep dragging you back to the cost of the system.

146

Reassure them of the benefits
The key is not to re-open the price negotiation; do not go back and start talking about price again – the price was working earlier, so stick to your guns. What you need to do is to reassure them of the benefits of your proposition:

- Summarise the business problem that the computer system will solve and seek confirmation that you have understood the problem correctly.
- Ask what the business implications are if the system is not installed and how the business will be affected.
- Establish the firm need and restate the benefits that your computer system will bring.

Make them feel the pain of not having the system and then restate the pleasure that they will experience by having the system installed.

CHECKLIST FOR GETTING IT RIGHT

✓ Have you sold the solution correctly? Make sure that they know what they are buying and the benefits it will offer them.
✓ Assess whether the technique is being used as a smokescreen or is a symptom of a genuine concern.
✓ Stick to your guns; don't re-open the debate on a point that you have already covered and agreed upon.

68

HOW TO HANDLE "... BUT MY HANDS ARE TIED"

'If they say they are sorry, do they really mean it?'

In many respects this is the most irritating and frustrating of obstacles you are likely to face. You believe you are coming down the 'home-stretch' on a deal, and suddenly you are up against "I'm sorry, but ...":

1. "... this goes outside my authority";
2. "... I need to get approval from the boss, and she's in hospital till the end of the week after next";
3. "... I've just discovered that my boss has been looking at one of your competitor's systems".

Everything before the 'but' A wise man once said that everything before the 'but' is bull. (As in ... "I think your system is terrific, but ...").

So, the first thing we need to ask ourselves is whether they really are 'sorry'. And if what they are saying is true. If it is not true, they are not a bit sorry.

The three examples given above were chosen to show three very different situations, though at first sight they may look similar.

1. Looks like simply a bit of stalling either to get some time to consider, or to get a second opinion from someone else in the company – authority or not. In this case, you might like to try a counter along the lines of, "Well don't worry: I do have another customer after it, and my next batch will be along in a month or two. You should be able to sort out the authority by then".

2. Has the hallmarks of truth. The word 'hospital' (few bosses are out of touch with their offices on overseas trips – even holidays), and the very specific timing given – even if it is maddeningly far off – are the clues. There is probably little point in trying to bluff some sort of rush into the system, except to make you feel better: "We're discontinuing this model, and you'll never see this price again". You never know: it might work. At least this will flush out the truth if they are bluffing. They may say, "Well let me try to place a call to her tonight, to see if I can get a decision".

3. Oh yeah? If competition bothered you, and if you didn't believe your product superior, you'd be in the wrong business ... "Fine! Let's go and discuss it with them".

Don't lose your temper Above all, keep cool and in control. Every fibre within you might be screaming "If your company has so little faith in your judgement that you have to put up your hand every time you want to pass wind, why have I been wasting my valuable time with a jumped-up office boy?" but you must hold it in till you can scream it at the rhododendron bushes at home. Never, under any circumstances, lose a customer for ever by losing your temper.

The way it works Software salesman Philip Hudson was nearly a victim of his own success, when he was trying to sell a data-security system to a branch of a building society. His price was so competitive that he knew his product was inside their own discretionary budget. The branch manager was so impressed with what he had been shown that he mentioned it to his area manager. The area manager passed the information upstream to his boss, and so on.

When Philip went to finalise the contract, the branch manager (who was a bit of a tease) told Philip that he had to make a presentation before some senior executives before the contract could be signed.

"I'm not the world's most patient man. I came within the thickness of a fag paper of telling him his fortune in four-letter words. But I took a deep breath and asked him why. It turned out that head office had been impressed by my specification sheets that he had faxed them. A few weeks later, I made my biggest sale, when the society put the system into all their branches."

CHECKLIST FOR GETTING IT RIGHT

✓ Take a good hard look at their excuse – it could be a bluff.
✓ If you think they might be bluffing, call them in the subtlest way you can come up with.
✓ NEVER lose control.

69

PREDETERMINE YOUR FALL-BACK POSITION – AND STICK TO IT!

'Decide the lowest you will accept.'

The problem associated with the expression 'fall-back position' is that it implies that you will be falling back! This is not the case. A so-called fall-back position is only a position from which you will not move. We might call this your strongest position or your calculated position or your best-case position, all infinitely better than ... fall-back.

For the sake of this section on negotiation, we will use calculated position as the most appropriate expression.

In any negotiation, someone usually has more at risk. This risk can be negated by proper planning, to ensure that each position in the potential negotiation has been examined and the consequence of accepting at each position has been fully worked out.

The best way to work out your calculated position is to examine the whole negotiation process from the other party's perspective, giving thought to the demands they may make. Those demands may well include concession or movement by you on the following:

- price;
- delivery terms;
- quantity price-points;
- payment terms;
- payment methods;
- financing;
- add-ons;
- timings;
- short-, medium- and long-term factors and arrangements; and/or
- outside influences.

In each of these areas, your calculated position should be examined.

Turnover is vanity ... Profit is sanity! An old expression but certainly true. Many negotiations have taken place in which the sole consideration in play was the price to be paid. This is not the most relevant factor. For anyone in business, it is the profit contained in each sale, in each deal, in each agreement that is really at stake. A 10 per cent reduction in price may well wipe out 50 per cent or more of the profit.

Consider the following example. Bennett & Company (Computers) Limited sell a range of networked computer systems with a nett profit of just 12 per cent after all expenses have been paid. One of their sales team is negotiating with a major customer for the sale of £150,000 worth of equipment. The profit of that sale would be just £18,000. A discount of 10 per cent on the sales price reduced the invoice to £135,000, however, and the profit reduced from £18,000 to just £3,000, hardly worth the time and effort taken, unless the sale was made for reasons other than initial profit. There are certainly occasions when an initial sale may not need to make a profit, for example, capturing market-share or capturing a prime customer in order to capitalise on the relationship over many years. If those or similar scenarios do not apply, take great care to ensure that profitability remains after the discount on the sales price.

The long-term impact

Discounts or pricing structures stated on a first sale may have long-term implications. Again, care must be taken to ensure that the purchaser is aware that any low price for an initial sale does not guarantee that arrangement on future business.

It's not the price – it's how you get there

Some years ago, I sent one of my managers on a negotiation course. He explained one of the key concepts he had learned in the following way. Two mock rôle-plays were undertaken: one was a long, hard battle on price and ancillaries, resulting in an agreed figure of £4,200; in the other, the person playing the part of the salesman accepted immediately the ridiculous first offer, just £2,000, of the rôle-playing buyer. The two who had played the part of the buyers in the rôle-play were asked for their reactions to the situations. The first, who had had the opportunity to haggle, felt pleased with the resultant price. The second, whose ridiculous offer has been immediately accepted ... felt cheated! The moral is clear – it's not the price, it's how you get to the price.

Two fall-back positions

It is often well worthwhile having two calculated positions. One, which for all intents and purposes, is your lowest figure and a second, known only to you, that may be a final position you would accept. If you get pushed to the limit on your calculated position, always, always ask for one further concession from the other side. This final point may well make that final position very acceptable.

 ## CHECKLIST FOR GETTING IT RIGHT

✓ Proper planning helps every negotiation.
✓ Calculate the real cost of all concessions.
✓ Turnover is vanity . . . profit is sanity.
✓ Always trade – never concede.

'Know your weak spot and it will be easier to conceal.'

Watch out for the jackals. In these 'caring' days of enlightenment and win-win outcomes, there can, sometimes, be a tendency to relax, let your guard down and be more open with people than you should. Unfortunately, there are those who will still take advantage of such openness and use privileged knowledge to better their own position. When this does happen, relationships break down, bitterness ensues and the business as a whole ends up paying the price.

Be careful in whom you confide, think about how what you say might be used in a different situation. Sad though it is, it's a fact of business life that these things are going to happen to all of us at some time.

Oops! – the way it works

Not convinced one of his largest suppliers was being straight with him, Brian Aston, production director of an East Midlands engineering firm, decided to take matters into his own hands. The developing dispute was over the price Brian was being quoted for specific materials. He was told that the price had been at this level for some time and, unfortunately, there was little more the supplier could do about it.

Upon being presented with this, Brian decided to telephone three of their other branches and request the same items, to see what they would say. To say he was stunned at his discovery would be an understatement. One of the branches was 18 per cent more expensive, whilst the other two were much less than his original price from his normal branch. Armed with this information, Brian once more contacted his branch asking, "Please can you help me? You said last week your price was fixed by your head office and that it is impossible to move on the cost price to me, even though we've dealt with each other for some considerable time. Why, then, when I ask three other branches is one more expensive and the other two a lot less?".

Silence, and an embarrassed individual at the other end of the line. Brian I'm pleased to say got exactly what he wanted, leaving the suppliers there to sort out how not to get caught like this again. How many times have we all seen this happen?

Spot it!

Now here's a tough one: how can you tell if someone is hunting for information they may well use in the future? These are just some of the ways others will get to know your deepest secrets; they may be helpful in making you aware of your surroundings and how careful you need to be:

- Firstly, be careful with what you say to strangers. Yes, that's obvious you say, but is it? Consider all of the places you meet people: offices, meetings, seminars, exhibitions, special events ... the list goes on; have you noticed just how quickly some people engage you in conversation?
- Know the people you are talking to. Even then, exercise caution: you don't know their hidden agenda or how what you allow to slip out can boost their cause.

- You must also watch what you put in writing; once it's gone out, it's too late to change your mind. Think, how would this look if it found its way here or to this person? People who are intent on building their own empires will use any and all means to pull the rug from right under your feet.
- Telephones are not always as safe for private conversations as we would like to think. Take care when using the other side's telephones; you never know who might be eavesdropping.
- Within your business, make sure your communication channels are open and information flows both ways; keep an eye on the accuracy and clarity.

Find your personal weak spot!
If you don't know what it is, please don't run away with the idea that one doesn't exist; it does and you, too, need to find it, before the other side spots it and uses it to their advantage. This happens all the time; it is essential *you* get the facts about you first. Try working with some of these ideas:

- Go to a professional to put you through some of today's personality tests. They don't have to be 100 per cent accurate but they will show a tendency which will provide you with some insight into the type of person you are.
- Talk to your boss: ask for a straight opinion on your skill/competency on the job you are doing, the purpose being that you have an external perspective on how other people see you. Do this with other working colleagues, to get a spread of views.
- Find out about the people you are about to sit around the table and negotiate with. Ask:

  - What is their expertise and experience?
  - How long have they been doing it?
  - What success do they have in doing what they do?
  - How have they dealt with something like this before?

- Know more about the other side than they know about you.
- Do your homework on the known areas the other side is most likely to want to know about; get supportive written evidence and put your points down in writing.
- Avoid discussing your private life; keep it professional.
- Most of the time it pays to be honest. If you're not a very convincing bluffer, tell the truth, to avoid the possible humiliation of their discovering your ignorance on a particular issue. That's the time you'll wish a hole beneath your feet would open up and swallow you!

 ## CHECKLIST FOR GETTING IT RIGHT

✓ Watch for jackals!
✓ When you discover someone else's Achilles' Heel, you have power over them.
✓ Find out about yourself before the other side does; they may just try to use something against you!
✓ Recognise the difference between *knowing* and *using* privileged information.
✓ Exercise care; what you give out surely comes back!

71 | TELEPHONE NEGOTIATIONS

'Listen to what is being said and how it is being said.'

Sometimes, negotiation by telephone is the only option, since time pressure or distance can make face-to-face negotiation impossible. Yet there are obvious difficulties in negotiating by telephone.

The importance of the visual image

As volumes of management literature will testify, vision is an extremely important communication medium. It is often said, for example, that we acquire 75 per cent of our information through sight, compared with about 16 per cent aurally. Denied sight of our opponent, we cannot benefit from body language, which can tell us so much.

Non-verbal communication

Of course, it is all too easy to misread the physical movements that people make and positions they adopt. When people fold their arms, they may be distancing themselves from us; they may also simply be adopting a more comfortable posture. Care is needed in interpreting body language but persistent types of behaviour, and particular changes in behaviour, can provide extremely useful information. For example, the following often hold true:

- Stroking chin – interested;
- Head leaning on hand – bored;
- Scratching top of head – confused or embarrassed;
- Steepling hands – poised and confident;
- Putting glasses down – stopped listening.

The fact is, that we are denied much useful information when negotiating by telephone. Worst of all, we cannot see the opponent's facial expression or their eyes.

There is also another factor to do with the proximity of another person, which affects communication and which makes it harder for either party to conceal the truth, although many succeed. Even the handshake has something to tell us.

Using the telephone

The telephone separates us from our opponent and makes it easier for one party or the other to conceal the truth. If you wish to conceal the truth, you may wish to negotiate by telephone; if not, always seek to negotiate in the presence of your opponent.

Nevertheless, it is worth pointing out that we do not lose all non-verbal communication when speaking by telephone. Pauses, the intonation of the voice, the register and quality of the voice, all tell us something about the other party. Whilst it is no substitute for sight, the fact that we cannot see the other person can help us focus on *what* is being said and *how* it is being said.

154

The real meaning

Of course, the words used are important but they are not always what they seem.

- 'Incidentally" or "by the way" often prefaces important information.
- "I don't wish to be personal, but ...," means the other person is about to be personal.
- "I'm no expert here, but ..." means the other person is probably about to give you a useful piece of information.

Negotiating by letter

If negotiating by telephone has major differences from negotiating in your opponent's presence, then negotiating by letter is different again. Here almost all the personality and non-verbal communication has been stripped away and therefore a very great deal has been lost. Nevertheless, there is also a gain.

A transcription of most people's speech would show an alarming number of grammatical errors and a considerable lack of precision. However, the written word will not allow these inaccuracies, and vague expressions and non sequiturs are often more obvious on paper. Nevertheless, the written word still requires interpretation, if only of what is not stated.

Not that old trick

Ronald and Barbara Walton owned a private school for 5–12 year olds in Suffolk. They wished to extend their resources, by purchasing and refurbishing two old buildings in northern France. These would be used for residential periods as part of the children's education.

They had identified the buildings during a week in which they had looked at various premises. Immediately after returning to England, they were telephoned by the estate agent in France responsible for selling the property. The estate agent explained that another purchaser had shown keen interest but they could have the property on a first- come-first-served basis. Neither Ronald nor Barbara were accustomed to negotiating and both accepted the message at its face value. They felt frustrated at having to decide immediately and they did not like agreeing in this manner by telephone.

They agreed to buy the property at the asking price. Thereafter, they always wondered if there had been another purchaser but they would never know. The likelihood is that they were encouraged to an early decision by an experienced negotiator.

CHECKLIST FOR GETTING IT RIGHT

✓ Be wary of someone trying to clinch a deal quickly by telephone.
✓ If possible, delay and seek a meeting.
✓ If a meeting is not possible, listen with extreme care and make notes.
✓ Listen to *what* is being said and *how* it is being said.
✓ Listen carefully for what is not being said.
✓ Avoid agreeing to anything in the first conversation. Say you will ring back.
✓ If necessary, supplement telephone conversations with faxed messages.

72 | PITCH IN QUICKLY AND BE THE FIRST TO SUMMARISE

'... seize the initiative.'

Every meeting needs someone to chair it. Who is it to be – them or you? The name of the game is control. Who is controlling the discussion? If you have any doubt, the one asking the questions is in control.

That's what the chair does – solicits the views of the people around the table. That's what you should do, even though there is only one other person around this particular table.

Once their cards are on the table, conclude the meeting

If you are on the selling side of the counter, you question the prospect on their requirements, question them on their budget and, when all their cards are on the table, conclude the meeting by telling them how both those criteria are going to be met by you or telling them that the only way they will satisfy that budget is by buying inferior goods (in which case, they may well try to 'unconclude' the meeting).

If you are on the buying side, you question the supplier on what they can provide, question them on what their prices are, question them on price concessions and, once all their cards are on the table, you conclude the meeting by telling them whether or not you are going to buy from them.

So there it is. What's the problem?

Are questions being fired to and fro?

Well, we all know that life is seldom quite as simple as that. For one thing, it might have dawned on the other side that questions are A Good Thing, so they may well be firing questions back at us. So the meeting will become a dialogue wherein questions are asked, answered with other questions, points are made, countered, re-made, re-countered, concessions are sought, reciprocal concessions are offered, and so on. But there will come a time when the discussion is in danger of becoming repetitive and sterile.

Before – not when – that happens, there is a vital initiative to be seized. It requires very precise timing but, if skilfully done, is immensely powerful. It takes control of the conclusion of the meeting – the most important part.

"OK, so let me sum up where we stand ...".

There will follow a précis, with the points made by both of you paraphrased. It may or may not conclude the deal but if it does not, it will set the agenda for the next meeting.

Make sure that it is you who does it.

156

Put yourself firmly in the driving seat

Why is it so important that this initiative be yours? Because it is an initiative, and initiative means control. It puts you firmly in the driving seat. It assumes chairmanship of the meeting. And the curious thing is that it does all this subliminally. You have not overtly assumed an authority over the opposition. You have been the one to take the trouble to – as it were – minute the meeting. But it gives you an intangible edge, a status, an earned respect, to which the opposition will subconsciously find themselves deferring.

This is very important indeed for the following reason (and, coincidentally, summarising is what I find myself doing now!)

The best deceiver does not win

In negotiation, we find ourselves playing with all sorts of devices, some of them extremely devious. It could, therefore, be assumed that, ultimately, it is the best deceiver who will win. This simply is not true. On the far side of the negotiation (assuming it is successful), there is 'doing business with ...'. For all the bluff and shadow-boxing in which we may have indulged, we are looking at an ongoing business association that will depend upon reliability, mutual trust, confidence and satisfaction.

Play the game as tough as you like, but never forget that the most profitable business to sell is repeat business. The best advertising is word-of-mouth. By all means, gain a reputation as a tough negotiator but also make sure that you are known as a straight one. Respect is the most valuable asset you will ever earn.

CHECKLIST FOR GETTING IT RIGHT

✓ When all their cards are on the table, conclude by telling them how their criteria will be met.
✓ If a deal is not concluded, summarising will set the agenda for the next meeting.
✓ Use a summary to take the lead and give yourself an intangible edge.
✓ Don't summarise to deceive – use it earn respect and future business.

INDEX

E 'ear pull' gestures **142**
'economical with the truth' ploy **142–3**
emotional fear **131**
emotions **47–8, 125**
   vengefulness **87–8**
empathy **49–50**
escape routes **92–3**
exclusivity deals **72–3**
experts **140–1**
extras **40–1, 60–1**
eye 'signals' **52, 62–3, 142**

F face-saving ploys **138–9**
'fake stalemate' tactic **12–13**
fall-back positions **92–3, 150–1**
fear factors **131–2**
'feel, felt, found' technique **85**
feelings *see* emotions
figures, bluffing with **25–6**
'final offer' tactics **111**
'final' points tactic **66–7**
financing questions **10–1**
flattery **140**
'floating' ideas **6–7**
'fly on the wall' perspective **8**

G gestures *see* body language
'getting your own back' **87–8**
'give and take' principle **136**
'goal post shift' ploy **30–1**
'going-in' positions **45**
'green light' signals **53–4**
'grinding down' tactics **74–5**

H 'hand over mouth' gestures **142**
'hands are tied' ploy **148–9**
'harping on the same old tune' **146–7**
humour **144–5**

I impression traps **34–5, 77**
'in tune', keeping **90–1**
'inadequacy' fears **131**
industry standards as precedents **107**
information
   gathering **8**
   power of **83**

initiatives, seizing **156–7**
instincts **115–16**
insults **47–8, 125–6**
intentional precedents **107**
intimidation *see* bullying tactics
intuition **115–16**

J 'just one more thing' ploy **66–7**

K know-it-alls **124–6**

L last-minute shifts **30–1, 66–7**
leading questions **17, 90**
'leaning towards/away' postures **52**
leaving tactics *see* walk-out tactics
leg crossing **51–2**
letters, negotiation by **155**
lies **27–8, 100–1, 142–3**
   bluffs **21–2, 25–6**
light asides **144**
'limited budget' ploy **111–12**
listening skills **142–3**
loaded questions **17–18**
'losing face' fears **131**

M 'making them sweat' ploy **120–1**
'manipulation' ploys **90–1**
market share questions **11**
mental maps **8**
'minimising concessions' ploy **109–10**
misinformation tricks **100–1**
mistakes **138–9**
misunderstandings
   as pretence **23–4**
modelling **35**
motivation issues **2–3**
'Mr Nice Guy' approach **98–9**
'multiple perspectives' approach **8**

N needs, wants compared **45–6**
network power **83**
'nibbling' **69**
'nice guy' approach **98–9**
'nice man, nasty man' ploy **81–2**
non-negotiable items **134–5**
non-verbal signals *see* body language

Free Special Report

(published price £14.95)

Which one would you like?

- ❏ Organise Yourself to be Lazy
- ❏ Clear Your Desk Once and For All
- ❏ How to Bankrupt a Rogue Company
- ❏ The Two Minute Presentation Planner
- ❏ Achieving ISO9000 - How much will it cost?
- ❏ Finding and Bidding for Bargain Properties at Auction

We would like to send you the Free Special Report of your choice.

Why?

Because we would like to add your name to our Business Enquirers Group – a selection of business people who receive regular information from us. We will offer you the best and most practical business books published, newsletters, a book review service and also offers from other companies with products and services that may interest you.

To order your free report and join the Business Enquirers Group, simply phone fax or write, give us your name, job title, address, phone, fax and e-mail numbers (if available) and quote MM02. And don't forget to tell us which report you want!

☎ 01353 665544

Ask for your free report by title and remember to quote our reference MM02

Fax 01353 667666

Photocopy this page, complete this box and fax it through to us

Name _____ Job title _____
Company _____
Address _____
_____ Post code _____
Phone _____ Fax _____ e-mail _____

Post

Wyvern Business Library MM02, FREEPOST CB511, Ely, Cambs CB7 4BR

Photocopy this page, fill in the box above (or staple your business card to it) and send it to us (no stamp required).